Loving Gifts from Heaven

Loving Gifts from Heaven

Comfort and Counsel from Loved Ones Above

Mary Shannon Bell, RN, MSN

Loving Gifts from Heaven:
Comfort and Counsel from Loved Ones Above
Copyright © 2010 by Mary Shannon Bell

Published by
Loving Gifts From Heaven, LLC
www.lovinggiftsfromheaven.com

All rights reserved. No part of this book may be reproduced, stored in a retrieval system, or transmitted in any form or by any means, electronic, mechanical, photocopying, recording or otherwise for private or public use, except for "fair use" as brief quotations embodied in critical articles and reviews, without prior written permission from the publisher.
For information and inquiries, address
Loving Gifts From Heaven LLC,
P.O. Box 1157
Middletown, MD 21769
or call (877) 371-2555,
or email info@lovinggiftsfromheaven.com

Library of Congress
Cataloging-in-Publication Data
is available upon request
ISBN-13: 978-0-9823908-0-1

First Edition, January, 2010

*In Loving Memory
of my parents,
Tim and Marty Shannon
I love you, Mom and Dad!*

"Normal People Are Boring"
C.C.
12 years old
August 28, 2007

CONTENTS

	INTRODUCTION	1
1	PENNIES—AND MORE—FROM HEAVEN	5
2	CHEESE CRACKERS	17
3	POTPOURRI	22
4	EVERYDAY ENERGY: TV, COMPUTER, PHONES & LIGHTS	33
5	DREAM VISITS	42
6	SYNCHRONICITY	49
7	GIFTS IN MY HEAD: IMAGES AND WORDS	55
8	SPECIAL SONGS	64
9	UNDER SIGNS AND WORDS	68
10	BIRDS AND FEATHERS	75
11	JOHN EDWARD—MEDIUM	78
12	GEORGE ANDERSON—MEDIUM	81
13	MARACAS	85
14	KEYS	87
15	ANGEL OF THE HEART	93
16	THE FINGERPRINT PENNY	95
17	CALLING HOME	97
18	RELIGIOUS SIGNS	100
19	BELIEFS	105
	EPILOGUE	109
	ACKNOWLEDGMENTS	111

INTRODUCTION

My parents in Heaven send me gifts—including coins that appear out of nowhere. Really. I wouldn't believe this if it hadn't happened to me (and many times). These coins and other loving gifts from my parents have helped heal my grief at their loss.

This book shares my stories of signs—which I also call gifts—from my parents and others in heaven. I have recorded gifts I've received for 5 years, since my dad passed. Having been the lucky recipient of too many signs to include in this book, I will only include my favorite ones, divided into various categories by chapters. Each chapter concludes with "hopeful hints" to suggest ways you can recognize your own signs from heaven. Just because we can't see those who have passed doesn't mean our loved ones in heaven aren't close at hand—they are.

I am neither a medium nor an expert on spiritual matters. In fact, I was a skeptic, a regular person who didn't believe in metaphysical phenomena before my dad passed. I probably would have laughed in disbelief about the contents of this book. Not anymore.

This book is written to help those in grief. As a registered nurse and one who wants to help others, I hope any who are missing loved ones in heaven will be comforted as they begin to recognize their own signs after reading about mine. The book may also enable non-believers to re-examine the possibility of afterlife communication as they consider the remarkable variety of signs sent by my loved ones to show that they are still around. As I tell friends, loved ones can't come down from Heaven and have coffee with us (as far as I know!), so they communicate with those of us still here on earth in any way they can. This book describes the many techniques they use to communicate. On our part, it's all about energy, awareness, and making connections. And it's about belief and faith too.

Months after writing the previous paragraph, I met a gifted medium who did not know that I often tell people the signs are subtle and those in Heaven can't come down for coffee. Even though she didn't know I tell everyone this, she immediately told me my father was behind me, coffee cup in hand, ready to talk. I just laughed—this sounded just like my dad and his humor!

The gifts come in all shapes and sizes. Sometimes they take the form of subtle signs, sometimes not. This book is not about seeing angels or the dead. It is not about dialogue between the dead and gifted mediums (although I do describe a few medium-related events). Instead, it is filled with different types of signs my parents in heaven use to communicate with me. Because the signs involve energy, some ways to communicate are easier to do than others. Many methods are universally used by quite a number of loved ones in heaven, such as flickering lights or visits to us as we sleep. The signs described in this book are mostly ones you might experience throughout your ordinary day—or night, in the case of dream visits.

Hopefully, those who read this book will realize their loved ones in Heaven are communicating with them and will start to see their own signs. Recognizing signs often will help comfort people and lessen their grief, as it has for me. Also, receiving signs helps us understand our loved ones are doing well in Heaven. Knowing this, in turn, can assist us to not miss them in the same ways and to move past our intense pain. I know this to be true for me.

Because my parents are at peace, still care about me, and are even with me at times, I have enough comfort in my heart to move forward with my life. When you recognize your loved ones are offering you comfort and counsel from above, perhaps you'll be able to step past your grief. Maybe you too will decide to try to live your best while here on earth, having learned that your loved ones in heaven really do survive their physical deaths. And perhaps you will come to know what I now understand: We are here such a short time before we rejoin them.

One way I want to live better is to give more, starting with these stories. These signs from heaven are gifts, and gifts are to be shared. I would feel negligent if I didn't pass on what has happened to me, knowing my experience may help someone else in grief. Also, it required a lot of energy from Heaven to send these gifts! Others should benefit from them too.

All it takes to start to receive these signs from Heaven is to open your heart, believe in and accept them. Asking those in Heaven helps too. As you do, I believe more and more signs will become apparent to you.

Receiving signs from Heaven is comforting beyond words. May you be healed by signs from loved ones in Heaven. And may these signs move you even more peacefully and joyfully through the remainder of your life here on Earth—until you see your loved ones again.

CHAPTER ONE

PENNIES—AND MORE—FROM HEAVEN

My parents send me pennies from Heaven. They also send me other coins: usually dimes, occasionally quarters, and rarely nickels. Since my dad passed five years ago, I have found around 900 (mostly pennies) coins in my path. George Anderson, a world-renowned medium—with no clues from me—confirmed that my parents, indeed, were sending me coins from beyond.

Sometimes pennies (or other coins) seem to appear out of thin air. I'll walk a few steps, turn around, and find a penny that wasn't there seconds before. Of course, my mouth drops each and every time a coin seems to have appeared out of nowhere!

Often I find coins under signs with words on them; these events will be described in another chapter. I have too many great coin stories for this book. My favorite coin stories will be shared here.

One of my most cherished penny incidents happened before Father's Day last year. I walked up to a display of gifts for fathers at the front of a Hallmark store and saw a picture frame with "I Love My Daddy" written on it. I thought "I wish there was a penny in it." Right then, I glanced to the floor to my left, and there was a penny! Without a doubt, this penny was not there a few seconds before. Thanks, Dad! *Good one.*

I first became aware of coins in my path early on after my dad passed. Often, I noticed coins on my closet floor, so I began to wonder how they got there after I saw more and more coins in my closet over time. I realized something unusual was happening.

One night, months after finding coins in my closet, I dreamed I was watching my husband and me sleeping in our bed. In this dream, a penny dropped from the ceiling and landed in the middle of our bed at the foot end. Not long after having this dream, I was unpacking a suitcase at the foot end of our bed; when I turned back to my suitcase, I found a penny on top of my next blouse to be unpacked! This penny was positioned exactly where the penny had hit the bed in my earlier dream! What is also unusual about this penny event is that I had not noticed the penny on the blouse after removing the clothes on top of it.

These next pennies-at-the-beach stories happened after my dad had been in Heaven four years, so it was easier for me to make the connection that the pennies were signs from my parents.

While enjoying several days at a sunny beach and boardwalk with my husband last July, I was reminded of many happy summer vacations at the beach in California with my family during the 1960's. My parents in Heaven must have been reminiscing too—because I found a lot of pennies from the 1960's in my path!

A 1966 penny, for example, was in front of our hotel next to a cardboard cut-out of a family at a beach. There were openings in the faces of the cardboard family members so people could put their own faces in the holes. This was comforting and funny at the same time: No longer in physical bodies as they "reside" in the spiritual world, my parents put a 1966 penny next to a cardboard family, as a way to show me they were with me as I remembered our 1960's family beach vacations. When I saw the penny there, I had to laugh out loud—and my parents knew I would. I love it when my parents' humor comes through loud and clear with their signs. It shows me they are doing just fine in Heaven, thank you very much.

While purchasing good walking shoes during this same beach vacation, the fit salesperson listened patiently as I actually told her I was such a fast 3 year-old toddler that my parents nicknamed me "Sputnik" in 1957 (after the Russian satellite that orbited around in circles). Less than two hours later, I found a 1957 penny directly in front of me on the ground.

Another precious, memorable sign given to me during this beach vacation was this one. I was walking along the shoreline one afternoon. First, I should mention that my daydreams occasionally include watching my parents—alive and young again—walking together at a beach shoreline with the waves to their right (I am behind them and to the left in my thoughts). Sometimes during these daydreams, my dad will turn around and show me a penny.

During the real beach vacation last July, while walking along the shoreline with the water to my right, I found a penny! It was on the wet sand, did not have sand on it, and would have been washed away by the next wave if I hadn't picked it up. I couldn't believe it. I found a penny while walking on the beach with the water to my right—it was exactly what my parents did in my daydreams. Once again, my mouth dropped. What's especially nice was how my parents were with me at the beach and during my daydreams. Thanks, Mom and Dad!

The next story is another time my parents showed me right away they were with me.

"South Pacific" was one of the old musicals my parents loved. It was one of many they enjoyed seeing on stage during the 50's and 60's in San Francisco. My siblings and I grew up singing all the old songs from these shows, including those from "South Pacific."

Pertinent to this story, by the way, is that both my parents served as United States Naval Officers during World War II. My dad, in fact, spent much of 1942 in the South Pacific.

Last December, I was singing songs from "South Pacific" while parking my car in a store parking lot. I entered the store and exited a few minutes later through the same door. I found a penny that had not been there on my way in. It was a 1942 penny! So, to summarize, I found a 1942 penny in 2008 outside a door where there had been no penny 5 minutes before—and I found this 1942 penny 7 minutes after singing songs from "South Pacific," where my father was stationed in 1942. What a special gift this was from my parents in Heaven. I felt them with me right when I realized it was a 1942 penny.

> Note: Valentine's Day 2013 - I had VERY deep, significant dream, received a 1996 dime, a ∞ small gold star, a 2006 AND a 1975 penny, + an elect. disturbance on computer w/ lem I hit "print" to a w/ lyrics of "Home". SIX gifts, at least.

It is noteworthy to mention that I find more coins around times of celebrations, such as family reunions, holidays, birthdays, or around the anniversaries of my parents' passing to Heaven. Here are some of my favorite recollections of finding coins around the time of such special days.

A once-in-a-lifetime-event was a family reunion for my dad's side of the family in July 2007. After leaving the family reunion, I found four pennies within 2-3 minutes—everywhere my eyes went, I saw a penny. I opened the car door, and there was a penny on the ground next to my car door. I walked into 7-11, stood in line, turned to my right, and there was a penny on the floor. Then I looked straight ahead and saw a third penny. Finally, after making my purchase, I walked toward the door and found a fourth penny.

The fast-paced timing of finding these pennies—4 of them within 2 minutes—just made me believe my dad was letting me know that he, my mom and others had been with us all at the reunion.

Another time I found a lot of pennies was during a trip to see my family in California. I had received other signs from above as well (which will be mentioned in other chapters). One coin event described below stopped me in my tracks.

Once back home at the airport, while waiting to meet my husband, I wondered if I would notice one more sign after having seen so many during my trip. My husband greeted me, and we walked to the car. There on the white line next to the passenger car door was a perfectly centered penny! Although I shouldn't have been shocked at this point because of all the signs I'd received during the trip (and the previous 3 years), I was. It was a perfect ending to a great vacation.

Before my wonderful niece's joyous wedding in September of 2008, I asked my parents in Heaven if they could drop a penny at the reception, to show that they were there. On the patio at the reception later on, I found a penny! It was, in fact, a tails 1983 penny. In my mind, a long time before my niece's wedding, I "designated" 1983 tails pennies I find as being coins from both of my parents (as you can imagine, I believe my parents know about my "designation" for tails 1983 pennies).

After this happy wedding, by the way, we were at the airport and there was a penny next to a security checkpoint box with these words written on it: "It's Magic." I often ask how all of these varied, otherworldly events happen. "It's Magic," is the answer!

Christmas was special for me while growing up, as it was for so many kids. My childhood memories of Christmas and the entire holiday season are precious. My siblings and I used to decorate the tree and house with my dad. Of course, my mom was busy Santa shopping for 7 kids, baking and cooking during this time. It is for these reasons, I believe, that I have found even more coins since my dad passed during the Christmas season. For example, once while looking at Christmas ornaments and lights at the back of a store (and nowhere near the cash registers), I found coins on the floor. One year after my dad passed, I found four dimes (each at a separate time) directly in my path on the same day! My parents let me know they were around me during these holiday times. It was very comforting. I don't grieve as much or as deeply around Christmas now.

Halloween was a celebrated holiday in our house as well. My dad thoroughly enjoyed the custom, traditions, costumes, candy, pumpkin (which he carved) and all else about Halloween. I like candy, and often joke that when I find these pennies from Heaven—I'm like a kid in a candy, I mean, coin store! Maybe my dad hears me saying this because, last Halloween, I found a penny with a small, clear candy wrapper on top of it! I just laughed. Another good one, Dad!

One day I parked my car on the fourth floor of a covered business parking garage. At the meter to insert my quarters (the meter only accepted quarters), I looked down on the ground near the meter and there were over 20 pennies! Where did these pennies come from? (I doubt a kid emptied a piggy bank up there) This event happened not too long after I began finding pennies and believing the coins were from my parents (but mostly my dad) in Heaven.

It was a beautiful spring day, and I was weeding in our backyard. I reached at least 2-3 inches down into the dirt to find the weed root. When I pulled the root up, there was also a penny in my hand! My dad always liked to garden and plant flowers.

After swimming many laps in a hotel pool in San Diego, I noticed a penny at the bottom of the pool that I hadn't noticed before. We played fun penny games in my parents' pool for many years.

While on business in Reading, UK, my husband found a U.S. penny on All Soul's Day. I just know it was from my parents or Frank's dad in Heaven.

Many times I have found Euros in my parking space after I have gotten out of my car—here in the U.S.! I like to think my parents gave me souvenirs from their travels. One of the last Euros was a 5 cent 2000 Euro, which shows the Cathedral of Santiago de Compostela, one of the most famous pilgrimage destinations in the world. I decided that my Catholic parents had just been there in spirit.

My husband and I found a penny on the U.S.S. Midway in San Diego. All four of our parents were U.S. Naval Officers during World War II. Perhaps my parents and Frank's father let us know they were with us as we toured this historic WW II ship.

Frank and I met his daughter, son-in-law, and grandson at an amusement park in Connecticut and there was a penny in our parking space. I have many fond memories of enjoying an amusement park called Paragon Park (which no longer exists) with my dad and relatives in Hull, Massachusetts. We had daily fun at Paragon Park while visiting my grandparents (my dad's folks) and our large family, 3,000 miles away from home during several summers in the 1960's. I believe my dad, on this summer day in 2007, let me know that he was there with us at this Connecticut amusement park by leaving a penny in our parking space. Perhaps he was remembering with me. It was a poignant moment.

Walking towards a MOM's Market (My Organic Market), I found a "Nebraska" quarter in my path on the ground. My mom was from Nebraska and I was about to enter the MOM's Market. Good one, Mom!

There have been times when I've opened my car door at a traffic light, out of curiosity, and have found pennies.

One morning, I was turning left into a parking lot and thinking about how I wouldn't believe all of these events were signs from Heaven had I not been finding these pennies so often. Right then, my eyes saw a penny in the street at the exact moment I said the word "pennies" to myself! The synchronicity of this event was unbelievable.

My husband and I were walking through the airport lobby once when we came across 56 cents on the floor! All coins but one quarter and one dime were pennies. Some pennies were rolling toward me! The kid in the candy, I mean, coin store in me just gleefully started picking them all up. My husband was close by, looking somewhat shocked (I've since recommended to him that he consider walking away and pretending he doesn't know me, should this happen again!). There was no one nearby appearing as if he or she had just dropped the money. Everyone was either sitting and reading, or walking by. I know, without a doubt, my parents orchestrated this event for different reasons.

After we sat down in our seats at the airport, I went to buy a paper. Upon returning to my seat, I found a cheese cracker (which is another sign from my dad that I discuss in the next chapter) near our seats and a penny underneath my chair. I was happy—thanks Mom and Dad!

Unpacking his suitcase the minute we reached our hotel room after a long drive, my husband discovered coins in the first dresser drawer he opened. There were 10 pennies. The word "Hi" was etched into the wood underneath the coins.

On the day before the 23rd anniversary of my mom's passing, two quarters seemed to "appear" on the ground in our garage. While looking at one quarter positioned a few feet in front of me, I tried to figure out how it got there (I always first try to make logical sense of any apparent signs from Heaven). Not having solved the mystery, I then walked up to the quarter, picked it up, turned around—and there was now a second quarter on the ground behind me! This second quarter wasn't there when I walked up to the first quarter. Momentarily scared, and wondering if I had been a witch in the 1500's, I remembered it was the day before the anniversary of my mom's passing. I was happy this quarter event happened 3 years after the start of receiving signs, because it would've scared me even more if it'd happened right after my dad passed.

About twenty minutes after finding the quarters, I received a sign of validation that these-appearing-out-of-nowhere quarters were connected to the anniversary of my mom's passing to Heaven the next day. I was holding our cat, Eamon, whom I've always thanked my mom and her sister, my Aunt Kathleen, for sending to us. Anyway, I was holding and loving Eamon in the garage (Eamon is never in the garage, which is almost a sign in itself)—right over the spot where I found the quarters!

One day, while leaving my car to enter a restaurant to meet my Aunt Millie, my dad's sister, for lunch—and it turned out to be the last time I saw her before she passed—there was a penny in my parking space.

The day before seeing my Aunt Millie, though, I went to Kinko's to print old family pictures to share with her at lunch the next day. Afterwards, I walked back to my car, put the pictures on the passenger seat, turned around, and saw a penny on the ground. The penny wasn't there when I arrived at the car. I had suspected for about two years prior to this event that coins can somehow appear out of thin air. Understandably, I could never accept such an idea. It was on this sunny day near Kinko's a few years ago, after printing pictures to show my aunt the next day when I was with her for the last time, that I realized coins can appear out of nowhere—and they are sent by loved ones in Heaven.

At the hotel, on the morning of my uncle's funeral (my dad's brother), I was in a little covered area between two sets of large glass doors. Stepping away for a minute, I returned to this area and found a quarter. Again, as mentioned in other stories: it wasn't there before (and no one had gone through the doors). To me, this quarter was placed between the two sets of doors by angels or loved ones above to symbolize my uncle's transition to Heaven on the day of his funeral. Having passed from Earth, he was beyond one set of doors and ready to go through the second set with his funeral. Perhaps the quarter would've been found past both sets of doors if discovered after, not before, my uncle's funeral.

One afternoon, my husband and I were sitting in the car, discussing how the pennies (that I had been finding for some time) could be from deceased loved ones. Most people are skeptical—including my husband. I said out loud in front of Frank, "Dad, please give me a penny when I go into the Safeway—maybe then Frank will believe me." I went inside the Safeway and the first thing my eyes saw was a penny on the floor! Frank, an engineer, was still not convinced the penny was from my father. That's understandable.

Having just seen the movie "Ghost Town" in October 2008, I found two dimes and seven pennies within an hour or so. My two parents had seven kids.

Speaking of kids, one day I received a brochure from a non-profit organization with words written similar to "...for a few cents a day you can be an angel to a child in need," and it had both a tails and a heads penny taped onto the brochure. Well, my parents sure have been angels to this child of theirs in her time of need!

At an outside mall one day, I tried calling my dad's doctor, with whom I'd spoken only a few times since my dad passed, just to say hello. He wasn't in the office. Minutes later, I walked by the same bench nearby where I had been standing when I tried reaching my dad's doctor, and there was now a penny! I believe my dad was letting me know he had been with me when I called his doctor to say hello.

Sometimes I've noticed coins under unusual items in the store. For instance, once there was a penny under the only item I went to purchase: mousetraps! Another time, a penny was in front of birdseed at the back of the Home Depot store—again, the only item I went into the store to buy. The penny, by the way, was underneath a different brand of birdseed than we usually bought, so I figured that those in Heaven wanted me to try a new brand. I did and the birds love it!

The most moving and loving gifts from my parents in Heaven have been given to me during my most intense times of grief since my dad passed five years ago. I am doing a lot better now, though, so what I describe next doesn't happen much at all anymore. In the past, I would find a penny within a minute or so after feeling very sad while missing my dad. In fact, once when I was really down, I found a penny with a paper heart right next to it outside my car door. How very loving and extremely comforting these incidents were for me. I realized more than ever that I was not alone. Of all the signs I've received since my dad passed, these have been the most healing and wonderful. Letting me know they were with me during my deep sadness helped me recognize what I'd heard: Love never dies. Thank you, Mom, Dad, Angels, and God.

Hopeful Hints

- Notice the date when you find coins in your path: Does it bring to mind a significant event in your life?
- When you find a coin, look at the year of the coin: Is it an important one for you or someone in your life (on Earth or in Heaven)?
- Jot down when and where you find your coins, their dates, and whether the coins were heads or tails: Can you spot any patterns?

CHAPTER TWO

CHEESE CRACKERS

My dad and I enjoyed snacking on cheese crackers, especially during the last few years of his life, and usually while playing the board game *Sequence*. It was a ritual—whenever I could be there: We would make something to drink, pour a bowl of cheese crackers, and play *Sequence,* usually around 5:00 PM in the afternoons. Sometimes we'd just eat some cheese crackers while watching TV. Others in the family enjoyed this routine with my dad as well. So, cheese crackers are special and personal crackers, as strange as that might sound, because they represent moments of being with my father.

Despite receiving all kinds of signs from both my parents (and anyone else) in Heaven during the first three years following my dad's passing, I still tried to explain strange events with my logical mind. So, when I first started finding single cheese crackers while inside department stores, bookstores, airports, for example, I just thought kids in strollers were accidentally dropping them. Eventually, though, what happened with cheese crackers was similar to what occurred with pennies—I came to believe my dad was leaving these cheese crackers for me to find. What cinched it for me that my dad was, indeed, "behind" these cheese crackers was what happened during the event described below.

I was in the Sport's Authority athletic store and spotted just one cheese cracker all by itself—usually the case for me. Who drops just one cheese cracker in weird places? More importantly, who finds only one cheese cracker as often as I do? No one does. Anyway, I saw the one cheese cracker and decided to take a closer look at where it was placed. It was underneath a rack of clothes, and at the top of the rack was a sign that read "Impossible is Nothing." That did it for me. The words even sound like my dad. I get it, Dad—thank you!

After finding the cheese cracker under the sign at Sport's Authority, on a different day I saw a single cheese cracker under a sign at the Target store with the words, "Target—Where Great Gifting Begins." The small, cheese crackers sure are "great gifts" for me—and personal, loving ones too, from my dad in Heaven.

While waiting in the left turning lane at a traffic light, I was gazing out the window when my eyes spotted a single cheese cracker at the end of the cement island to my left! Who crosses intersections, stops on the island in the middle of the street, and drops a single cheese cracker? Once again, no one does.

Another time I came out to my car in a hotel parking lot to find a single cheese cracker near the passenger door. It wasn't there when I exited my car the previous evening.

One day, I walked into the MOM's Market and immediately saw one single cheese cracker on the floor near the register. I asked the clerk if they sold these particular cheese crackers. Initially, she said yes, but when she tried to take me to where they sold them, she realized the store did not carry them. I knew they didn't sell them right when my eyes spotted the cheese cracker. This is one of my mom and dad's ways of removing the doubts that arise in my mind—by leaving these little cheese crackers, for example, in places where they're not sold.

Safeway had its Easter candy on display at the front of the store one April. Easter (and the candy associated with it!) was special to me while growing up. One day I found a single cheese cracker underneath the exact candy the Easter Bunny left us on Easter mornings when we were young.

My husband and I checked into a hotel at Lake Tahoe after another wonderful niece's wedding. I had been finding coins and other signs quite a bit during the trip. My husband opened the car door after we parked and found a penny where he put his foot down. Less than five minutes later, we got into our hotel room and there was a single cheese cracker on the otherwise spotless rug, just a little out of the way so the housekeeper missed it. There were no cheese crackers for sale in the room's mini bar, by the way.

While at the pharmacy on a day when I was feeling down about missing my dad, I came across a single cheese cracker at the start of the "First Aid" aisle, under boxes of "First Aid" bandages. Because of its location, the cheese cracker did make me feel better.

As I was writing this chapter, I had a few different cheese cracker incidents occur that I believe were given to me for the purpose of spicing up this chapter!

Recently, I found a cheese cracker at the beach…and it was tan! It was a wheat cracker, but I'd never seen one like this before. Finding a tan-colored one for the first time while at the beach is an example of both my parents' sense of humor at work (or at play, if you will)!

Here is another cheese cracker story that "showcases" my dad's sense of humor. I have received many eagle-related signs over the last few years (I discuss these signs in another chapter). One day, I was outside a Swarovski's crystal store, admiring the very large crystal eagle in the display case. It was next to many other crystal animals showcased as well. Connected to this case was a floor-length empty window. I looked into this large window—and there by its lonesome self on the rug was a single cheese cracker! I just started laughing—it was as if this cheese cracker wanted to be displayed alongside the animals. This was another time when I said, "Good one, Dad!" My dad knew I'd laugh and know it was him having fun with me. I just *love* seeing proof my father is so *healthy* on the Other Side, evidenced by the many displays of his great sense of humor.

My dad has helped me come to believe that fun and joy are a huge part of these afterlife communications. In fact, one time I found a cheese cracker all by itself under a greeting card with these words: Just for Fun.

I have saved my two favorite cheese cracker stories for last.

In Barnes & Noble bookstore one day, I cut through an aisle, and saw something orange out of the corner of my eye. I looked down and there was a single cheese cracker—directly beneath four Bibles! Looking up to the shelf above, I saw a bible titled *Dad's Bible: The Father's Plan*, by Robert Wolgemuth.

Finally, the day I started this book, I asked for a sign that would show me I was on the right track writing this book. After working on my notes for a while, I took a break and went to the store. The market had large boxes of cheese crackers stacked at the end of an aisle. There in front of all those huge cheese cracker boxes was a penny! I could not believe it! Two big signs from Heaven—a penny and cheese crackers—had been combined. I believed it was the sign from Heaven I had asked for earlier to know if I was to continue on this path. And recently, I found a dime underneath small boxes of cheese crackers. I am convinced these events are signs from my dad in Heaven.

Hopeful Hints

- Look for a connection between a physical item in your path (especially one found often) and your loved ones in Heaven: What does it mean to you or to them?
- Is the location of an item (a gift from Heaven) an unusual or meaningful one? Might this location signify a special message for you?
- Remember your loved ones in Heaven are full of joy and may be trying to make you feel good through their gifts: Does the sign make you think of them and smile or laugh? Is the location of the gift amusing in a way that helps you recognize your loved ones in Heaven are behind it?

CHAPTER THREE

POTPOURRI

I have received so many material, or physical, gifts from my parents which were neither coins nor cheese crackers over the last five years. Rather than name this chapter "Non-Coin Material Gifts," I've re-named it "Potpourri" to reflect a mixed collection of signs or gifts from Heaven. As with the coins and cheese crackers gifts, I will write only about my most memorable ones.

I received a sign from my dad in a dream the night before his first birthday after he passed. In the dream, I told him how much I missed him, and he said, "I know." I was so happy—and lucky to receive such a treasured gift from my dad on *his* birthday. My husband and I were in Ireland at the time. Although I felt very grateful to have received a loving dream visit while we were in my ancestors' home country—my Irish maiden name is Mary Shannon—I hoped to receive another sign during the daytime on my dad's birthday while In Ireland.

So, I asked my parents for another sign. This is what happened later that day. My husband and I had been to beautiful St. Patrick's Cathedral a few days before, but on this day, I decided to stop by St. Patrick's Cathedral again to buy a souvenir at the gift shop. This is an example of my doing something differently than planned, so I would unknowingly be in a position to receive a sign from Heaven.

My husband did not come inside the very pretty cathedral this time because I was only going to be inside for a few minutes. Once inside, I turned around, looked toward the gift shop, and saw my requested sign from Heaven! Facing me were two ceramic nameplates next to each other on a spindle rack. The two nameplates read: "Mary Shannon." As I mentioned, my maiden name is Mary Shannon. I looked up and said, "Thanks, Dad and Mom, and thanks God." Of course, I bought the nameplates. (What are the odds, by the way, that those 2 names would be next to each other?)

Speaking of Irish things, I received a free book in the mail titled *Rainbow's End* by Irene Hannon the day before St. Patrick's Day.

Not long after my dad passed, a gift from my dad was right in front of my foot when I got out of the car one day. There was a big silver object, and even before picking it up, I knew it was for me. (I know how that sounds, but I've just had too many things happen! Also, my intuition helps.) It was an unbroken Hallmark keychain medallion. The medallion had the following written on it: "Boston—Where It All Began." The medallion listed all of Boston's tourist sites. The other side of the medallion had a picture of Boston Harbor. My dad was born and raised in Boston. As I mentioned in my coin chapter, my dad took a few of us kids back to Boston from California each two or three summers to visit his parents. My dad visited his folks every few years for decades, until his parents passed. While in Boston, my dad would take us to most of the tourist sites listed on this medallion I found right outside my car door. Also, written on the medallion was: "These are only a few of Bean Town's many treasures." No kidding, Dad! You are the best Bean Town treasure there ever was! What a *gift*—thank you, Dad!

My wonderful dad, by the way, was named Timothy Joseph Shannon, after his grandfather. His dad was Joseph Leo Shannon. My dad was known as "Joe" by all while growing up. An excellent student and very knowledgeable about quite a few subjects, he practiced dentistry for over 36 years. My parents had many admirable qualities, for which they both will always be remembered. Back to my signs.

It was 3 years after my dad passed when I began to notice more varied signs from Heaven. Also, I began to realize more than ever the signs were all about energy. I believe my conclusion was validated when I parked the car and saw something small in the space next to mine. My intuition led me to look at the item. It was just one Pokemon card with the word "Energy" written on it. The card had the image of fire on it. My astrological sun sign is Sagittarius, by the way, and my symbol is fire. (Just for the record, I never believed in anything related to astrology before I started receiving signs from above).

Out of the blue one day I decided to wear my socks with butterflies on them—to work, mind you—ones I never wore anywhere. Later on, at the bookstore I saw Allison DuBois's new book titled: *Secret of the Monarch: What the Dead Can Teach Us About Living a Better Life.* On my way to the front of store to buy it, I found a shiny dime directly in my path.

Another butterfly incident happened at Starbucks on a different day. While walking toward the Starbucks' door entrance, I noticed a man and presumably his young daughter looking at a bush about 15 feet away. They turned around and looked at me. It was then I noticed the butterfly they had been watching had flown over to my vicinity and was circling my head.

I received a sign while sorting through my dad's photos after he passed. But, to better understand the following sign from Heaven, I need to mention that my dad, a classical literature scholar, was referencing Aristophanes' play "The Frog" while in the hospital toward the end of his life. It is a very old play written by a Greek author in the 1700s, and most people aren't familiar with it, unless they're classical literature enthusiasts too. (There is a reason why my dad was referencing this play, which is another unrelated story.) Anyway, after my dad passed, I was dividing up his photos per his written instructions, and I took a break for lunch. While eating, I opened up "The New Yorker," my husband's magazine, one I never read (this is another example of my doing something I don't normally do so I would receive my sign from the Other Side). After opening "The New Yorker," my eyes went straight to the middle of the page where I immediately read "The Frog—by Aristophanes." This obscure, unknown play was being performed in New York.

My opening "The New Yorker," which I never do, while taking a break from organizing my father's photos, and my eyes immediately seeing "The Frog," an almost unheard-of play, led me to believe my dad was with me as I reminisced while looking through the old pictures. It was a moving moment—and a tearful one.

Another sign involving magazines occurred one day at a bookstore. I was walking by a chair and felt very drawn toward a magazine insert lying on the chair. (I don't ever get magnetically drawn to things, especially not magazine inserts!) I looked at it and read the words, "Live to the Edge of Your Imagination." I couldn't believe it.

One day I opened my car door and right where I put my foot down was a sparkling jewel that looked exactly like a diamond! Although it looked like one, a jeweler confirmed that it was a zirconium (darn). A half hour before this zirconium encounter happened, though, I saw something that looked like a diamond near my car at a different parking space. This event was very strange for me: I questioned whether I had possibly seen a diamond in one spot, and then later found a zirconium outside my car door in another parking space.

While in Las Vegas, Nevada for a nursing conference, I walked by a penny slot machine that had the image of a Native American on it, along with the word "Spirit." I joked to my friend that maybe my Spirit Guide would help me win. After inserting a few pennies, the machine began lighting up and making noise for several minutes. I won $120.

Scrolling down the "Messages from Beyond" page on psychic medium, Lisa Williams' website, I read: "Mary—We're with you and love you. Love, Mom." Prior to reading this message on that day, I had come across an old e-mail someone had written to me where she had mistakenly signed it "Love, Mom." So, I like to think I received two messages from my mom in one day—the e-mail that was signed "Love, Mom" and the message on Lisa Williams' website. Prior to this day, I believed I had received communication from my parents in the form of words written in my head, so I believe writing words is a method of communication my parents—my mom, in particular—use to communicate with me from the Other Side.

I bought flowers for my husband the day before his birthday a few years ago. I put them in a tall vase on a placemat on the nook table. Forgetting the flower vase might be knocked over by our cats, I did not move the vase to a safer location before going to bed. The next morning my husband asked me, "Honey?" in a strange voice. As I walked into the kitchen, he showed me his vase of flowers standing on the same placemat on the nook table, just as we left it the night before. But now the vase was only half-full of water, the placemat was wet, and there was water on the floor! Neither my husband nor I had moved the flowers or, more importantly, had spilled water out of the vase.

The question wasn't: Who knocked over the flowers? Of course, the cats must have done it. The question was: Who lifted the vase back up that obviously had been knocked over during the night?

I believe, of course, that it was a group effort by many loved ones in Heaven: my parents, my husband's father, and the couple who gave us the vase (all of whom are in Heaven now). They worked as a team to put up my husband's flowers. They all wanted my husband to come into the kitchen on his birthday morning to standing birthday flowers, darn it! But they had to rectify the situation because the cats had knocked over the vase. This gesture of caring about the flowers was such an expression of love to my husband on his birthday. I do wonder, though, how many spirits and angels it really took in total to up-right such a heavy vase!

While on the train traveling to my uncle's funeral, my dad's brother, I was picturing the two of them playing the *Sequence* board game in Heaven. Upon arriving at the train station, I stepped off the train, walked a few feet, and there on the ground was a royal blue disc, one very similar in appearance to the royal blue player piece used in *Sequence*. I know in my heart that my dad put it there, just like all the pennies, dimes, and other gifts I have found. My dad showing me this blue disc in my path moments after exiting the train let me know that he was aware of what I had been picturing in my mind—my dad and uncle playing *Sequence* in Heaven.

I believe when picture frames fall over in the home, this is a sign from those who have passed. Loved ones in heaven are able to knock things over onto the table or floor. This is what I felt happened when I walked into a Hallmark store right after it opened for business. No one else had entered the store, but there was a card on the floor: It was a Valentine's Day card for a daughter. The store had just opened, so everything should've been off the floor. But only one card was out of its rack—a loving card for a daughter.

While sitting on the ground near the Truckee River in Lake Tahoe, I looked right beside me and found a medallion that said "Eagle Hawk," along with a few other words. Since finding this medallion, I've had other eagle-related incidents, as I mentioned in the previous chapter, and will talk about more in a later chapter.

On another vacation, I found a silver-plated ring with an ancient design of some type etched onto it. It didn't appear to have been worn recently, as it needed to be cleaned. It fit me perfectly. The ring had a small eagle in the design.

Although some of the following signs could be saved for another chapter, I have decided to add them here because the signs involve material gifts that aren't coins.

By my bed, I have a Book of Psalms for the calendar year. A different psalm is provided for each day of the year. Unfortunately for me, I rarely open it. One night, nine months after my dad passed, I uncharacteristically felt like opening the Book of Psalms. I opened it to the current day, and the Psalm for that day was Psalm 23. This is the Psalm beginning with "The Lord is my Shepherd, I shall not want." Our family had Psalm 23 placed on my father's mortuary card, and it was also sung during his church service.

One day I went to the YMCA to swim and there were two religious pamphlets by Project Restore, Inc. in my locker (ones I couldn't find anywhere else at the YMCA that day). They were titled: "A Love Stronger Than Death: Mysteries of the Great Beyond," and "A Time for Joy: A Day to Remember." The second pamphlet had a pink rose on it, which has been said to represent love from the Other Side.

The following event happened four years ago, not long after my dad passed. At the time the incident occurred, I did not believe it was a sign from Heaven meant for me, but now I wonder. On this particular day, I drove under a freeway overpass with a chain link fence, and attached to the fence were red balloons that formed the words "LOVE YOU MARY." As I said, I didn't think the message was for me back then, but it made me feel better—and I did have fun pretending the red balloons were for me. But even at that time, I wondered to myself: Younger people put balloons and signs on fences for their similarly young friends, but how many younger people are named Mary these days?

Now, five years later and after receiving words in my mind written in red letters—and after receiving so many gifts from Heaven—I wonder if the balloons actually were for me.

Nowadays, I find small batteries and paperclips all the time and in the most unlikely places. Once I went to the photo store to look for a camera battery, and when I came back to my car there was a small battery near my door. It wasn't there when I got out of my car. The significance of finding so many batteries in my path could be "it's all about energy." Perhaps the paperclips represent writing (and completing!) this book.

Similarly to finding batteries, I also find small electrical converters—and with coins appearing next to them! I was walking through a large empty parking lot and came across a small electrical converter for a headset or computer. As I walked by it again five minutes later, there was a dime right next to it! No cars had parked nearby within these five minutes. I know the dime hadn't been there just a few minutes earlier.

Maybe those on the Other Side were letting me know they were aware that I would be writing this chapter and the next one—both are about electricity and energy. But now, months after first starting this chapter—and after many more events and gifts from Heaven—I believe the underlying message was that *all* of the signs—including receiving coins—have to do with *energy*.

Before Christmas 2008, I was talking with someone about how I believe my parents give all six of my siblings signs from Heaven as well (I'm not singled out). Shortly after this conversation, I returned to my car with a newspaper and put it in the back seat. Then, just moments later, I realized I wanted to go back to the store. I opened the car door and there was now an ad on the ground. I don't believe I dropped the ad from the newspaper, but maybe I did (if I had to bet, I'd say I didn't drop it). So I looked at this Sam's Jewelry ad and on it was printed the dollar amount of $526 under a picture of a diamond cross. My dad passed on 5/26. Not only that, just below the cross selling for $526, the ad read: "Some gifts money can't buy." When I first saw the ad on the ground, I thought there was only one. I then discovered there were seven of these ads, perfectly stacked on top of each other. Seven. My parents had seven children—gifts money can't buy.

First, I don't believe I dropped the ads out of the newspaper. Second, even though there are often a few of the exact same ads in a newspaper, I have never found seven copies of the same ad. Third, these ads were perfectly stacked on the ground, and how could that have happened if they had fallen out of my newspaper from above? Fourth, the ad had the date my dad passed under a diamond *cross*, with "Some gifts money can't buy" printed on each of the precisely stacked *seven* ads (one for each of my parents' seven kids), right before Christmas. Fifth, I had just recently talked with someone about how I believe my parents give signs to each of my siblings as well. This sign was so incredibly special for me, and it happened around Christmas, a time when I appreciate even more the gifts from my parents in Heaven.

One of the most special gifts I've received from the Other Side—specifically from my mom and any helpers she may have—was one I was given after she passed, over 20 years ago. Of course, at the time I was given this gift, I didn't think my mom in Heaven was involved. Now I believe with my whole heart my mom was behind it.

My mother, Martha Ann Morrow, known and loved by all as "Marty," was the 1938 May Queen at the University of Nebraska, a large Midwestern school. This was only one of my mom's great honors and achievements during her college years. I was always proud of my mother for many reasons. This was one reason. Growing up, I was able to admire a large, framed photograph of my mom as May Queen displayed in our house. I was never able to see my mom's May Queen picture in her 1938 college yearbook, however, because the school put the picture of the 1938 May Queen in the 1939 yearbook. My mom didn't have the 1939 yearbook. Still, I always wished I could have seen my mom's May Queen picture in the 1939 yearbook.

Fast forward to 1988, fifty years after my mom was May Queen, and I was working as an Occupational Health Nurse at a semi-conductor company. A physician, who was conducting employee physicals, and I were talking about our parents. It turns out his parents were born a few years after my mom, and they also graduated from the University of Nebraska.

The next day, this very nice man came in with both the 1938 and 1939 University of Nebraska yearbooks to give to me as gifts from his parents! I'd always just wanted to see the 1939 yearbook so I could admire my mom's May Queen picture. Here I was, though, not only seeing it, but receiving the 1939 and 1938 yearbooks as gifts. I continue to thank this thoughtful doctor, his generous, kind parents, my wonderful mom, and God! I just know my mom orchestrated this event. Thanks, Mom!

Finally, one day my parents' Mass cards, which I keep in my purse, were misplaced. I later found them in my address book. My interpretation as to why I finally found the Mass cards in my address book was this: My parents are with each member of their family, including 7 children and 11 grandchildren, at the same time. Thanks, Mom and Dad, for all of these wonderful gifts!

Hopeful Hints

- *Be on the lookout for an ordinary object that seems to disappear and then reappear: where do you finally find it? Is the location significant or symbolic?*
- *Do framed photos of your loved ones in Heaven fall over for no reason at all? Are they just saying "hello," or is there something special about the day the photo falls over?*
- *When you frequently observe the same item everywhere you go, ask yourself: is there is a very dear connection between the object and your loved one in Heaven?*

CHAPTER FOUR

EVERYDAY ENERGY: TV, COMPUTER, PHONES & LIGHTS

Many psychics, mediums, and others say those in spirit can affect electrical lights and equipment in the home as they communicate with us. This is just one of their many methods of communication. I believe this to be true, but again, wouldn't have believed it unless all kinds of unusual electrical events hadn't occurred in our home. There are too many incidents to discuss in this book, but the following are some of the most memorable electrical events that have occurred since my dad passed, involving everything from television and telephones, to clocks, computers, and lights.

The day I began writing this book, for example, I was typing on the computer keyboard. After I typed the word "Dad," the computer "d" key kept making more "d's"! My hands were off the keyboard, the "d" key wasn't stuck, and this did not happen again.

Another computer-related incident occurred when I was reading an e-mail one day. My hand was on the computer mouse and, without any effort on my part, my hand and cursor moved up to a sentence in the e-mail about "letting people know." This happened after many other incidents had occurred, leaving me with the feeling that I was supposed to let others know about all of the unusual events that had happened—ones I believed were signs from my parents in Heaven.

On May 24, 2007, two nights before the third anniversary of my father's passing, my husband arrived home with a bouquet of lovely pink roses, and they were a welcomed, wonderful surprise. The vase of pink roses was the only item on our kitchen island. The three recessed lights above our kitchen island were turned on, as were other lights in the nearby nook and family room.

After my husband had gone to bed, I was in the kitchen when the three recessed lights above the vase of pink roses on the island went out—and I hadn't switched the lights off! No other lights or electricity went out. The recessed lights stayed off for about 3-4 seconds, before they came back on. After the lights were back on, the middle recessed light flickered several times, reminding me of a sparkler on the 4th of July. And then all three lights stayed on. I am writing this one year later, and we have not had to change any of those recessed lights, nor has that "light show," as I call it, occurred again. Looking back, I believe it's possible that the middle light flickered three times as a way to signify each year since my dad passed, as the third anniversary of my dad's passing was in two days.

Special note: Since the time I wrote the above paragraph, my dad's brother passed on May 12, 2008. The day he passed, the middle recessed light—the one that had flickered 3 times nearly one year before, right before the third anniversary of my dad's passing—burned out.

On the day my uncle passed, I was at an office when the electricity went out for a short awhile—including all of the recessed lights.

I will now share my favorite "phone" signs from my parents. I was looking at a map of Ireland when my home phone rang and the caller ID showed my own cell phone number. I had my cell phone on my belt but hadn't picked it up or even accidentally touched it. So, after seeing my cell phone number on our home phone's caller ID, I looked at my cell phone, which has our home number programmed into it, and my cell phone read "Home." Again, I'm looking at a map of Ireland, where my ancestors are from—and perhaps where I lived in another life, who knows—and my cell phone reads "Home." I could not believe it.

I describe a very special, incredible sign involving phones in a later chapter titled, "Calling Home." It occurred after attending a wonderful event led by the very gifted, famous psychic-medium, Allison DuBois. I won't share more now, only because I don't want to repeat myself.

Today, one of our regular land line phones rang in the kitchen. The message on the caller ID display said, "Call from base." When the phone rang, it sounded different. Neither the cats nor I had touched the phone. I can't explain how it happened. But I find it interesting that it occurred on this day, as I was writing the chapter on phone signs!

After writing about the unusual event in the above paragraph, I took a short break so I could look through my documentation of my telephone signs from Heaven. As I was looking through my files, the office phone rang once. The ring sounded odd like the one in the kitchen had—it was more like an alarm clock ring than a phone ring. This hadn't happened before today with any of our home phones. But, here I am, writing about "phone signs" in the chapter on "electrical gifts."

Looking at my cell phone one day, it read "POP7." My dad was father or "Pop" to 7 kids. I tried, but couldn't reproduce this on my cell phone, although it can be done. How it showed up on my phone, I can only guess.

Recently, I opened my bedroom door while I was talking on my cell phone. Right at the exact moment I opened the door, our house electricity went out and my cell phone died! The "coincidence" of my opening the door right when the electricity went out is remarkable timing, but my cell phone died right then too. I never looked into it, but I will bet the cell phone tower did not lose power right at the same time the electricity went out. Although I cannot understand how both the electricity and cell phone went out at the exact same time, I believe the event was orchestrated from Heaven.

As I move into sharing the incidents involving television, I want to say again that I believe the communication gifts I receive from the Other Side are mostly orchestrated by my dad.

I never watch TV on weekend afternoons, but something made me want to turn on the TV one Saturday afternoon. So, I turned on the guide channel and saw that one of my favorite movies, "Ghost" with Demi Moore and Patrick Swayze, was showing at that time. I had been finding pennies for a few years by this time. The very first image on my TV, after changing the channel to "Ghost," was a huge penny! And it filled the entire TV screen! (It was the scene where Patrick Swayze makes the penny move up the door, into the air, and over to Demi) But, again, the first thing I saw when I changed the channel to this movie was a full-screen penny. Good one, Dad! I just know my dad got me to turn the TV on right then so I would see this familiar sign from him: a penny.

Not long ago, I was extremely drawn toward turning on the television at an odd time and with a sense of urgency (it was as if I heard "hurry!"). Moments later, I heard singers on the Lawrence Welk show begin to sing a song about San Jose. The PBS station was playing an old Lawrence Welk California vacation theme show. Another song about San Francisco was sung on this show as well. My parents met, fell in love, and married in San Francisco. They brought up all seven kids (including me) in San Jose. And they loved watching the

Lawrence Welk show! Without a doubt, I know my parents wanted me to hear the beginning of the San Jose song, and that is why I felt I needed to hurry up and find the right channel!

Once, an advertisement came on while I was watching TV. It was for a new movie and the plot had something to do with "stars." During the advertisement, I saw a rectangular, horizontally-positioned white box with the name "Mary" inside—and written in red letters. This white box was in the upper right corner of my screen. The only other significant thing about this box, besides it having my name in it, is that it was there! I mean, I don't think this small white box with my name in it was part of the movie's TV ad. It didn't look like it "fit" either. Also, I looked up the movie, and there was no mention of "Mary" that I could find. The box was only momentarily on the screen, and then the ad picture changed. Perhaps those above made use of an opportunity to communicate with me through an easier medium—TV.

One night the television was on while I was reading a book. "American Idol" was about to start. The TV was on Channel 5, which airs "American Idol." After a moment, I looked up from my book and my TV screen was black, but the TV's green power light was still on. I pressed the guide button on the remote control, and the guide did not show the TV to be on Channel 5 anymore. The TV guide was highlighting a PBS (Public Broadcasting Station) channel and a description of the program that was being aired on that channel: "Secrets of the Dead—The Story Behind the Creation of the King James' Bible from Mysterious and Inaccessible Latin Texts to a Book for the Common English-Speaking People." My father, who was religious and a Latin scholar, knew Catholicism very well. Perhaps God and others besides my dad were behind this sign—they all know I sure need help with the Bible!

While trying to change the TV channel using the remote control to "Law & Order: Criminal Intent," I noticed that the TV was on a religious station that I never watch—a station I didn't even know we could access.

Another time, a TV show about a psychic detective called "Raines" was on. To summarize the storyline, Raines did not admit to the police psychiatrist that he could actually see and communicate with the dead. Later on, at the end of the show, a girl who had passed was with Raines. When he asked her why she was still there since he had solved her murder, she replied, "Tell them that you see us."

Then, all of a sudden, at the same time this little girl was saying, "Tell them that you see us," a bluish light started moving from the right lower corner of my TV screen toward the center. This bluish light grew larger before turning into a white light. But it did not become so large that it filled the TV screen. As it was happening, I didn't understand why or if it had to do with the show. But then I realized the light was increasing in size just as the little girl was saying, "Tell them that you see us."

I know the light was happening to the TV, not the show. Light—which many believe is a way spirits can be seen—was expanding on the television screen as I was hearing a TV character on the Other Side say, "Tell them that you see us." This occurred after receiving many, many signs. I made the connection. And I am trying to tell people with this book.

One year after my dad passed, and just before Christmas, my husband was traveling and I was alone in the house. A Hallmark movie called "The Christmas Visitor" was on TV. It was about an angel who helped a grieving family celebrate Christmas, as the family members hadn't celebrated in years since their son had passed. Toward the end of the movie, one of the daughters in the movie said,

"I'm okay." Right then, my TV went black. I immediately looked at my TV control and the first place my eyes landed was on the button that says "OK." I believe it was a message from my dad, saying: "I'm okay, okay?"

It's not unusual for my TV to go black for no apparent reason when my husband is traveling. It's not scary to me because I believe my parents are letting me know that they are with me while Frank is away. Often what happens is the TV screen will turn black but the green power light will remain on. Then a few moments later, the TV screen comes back on.

After feeling a little discouraged about something one day, I flipped through the TV channels and came across a show with the following brief description in the guide section: "Mary's father offers encouragement."

Another time while watching TV, the TV seemed to change channels on its own. It's possible that I accidentally hit the control, but I don't believe I did. The next thing I heard was "when I met your mother." I wondered if the sign had anything to do with my dad meeting my mom again—in Heaven.

One day, the TV was on while I was not really paying attention, when the screen suddenly changed to a blank white screen with numbers 1–6 written in a vertical column. Next to each number was the word "channel." After I read this, the TV went back to its regular program again. I had not touched the TV channel control. I believe the reason this event occurred (as well as some others not mentioned) was so I would receive a message about metaphysical-type channels.

I will share a few more signs from Heaven involving electricity. On July 4th a few years ago, before watching the fireworks on TV with my husband, I went into a room, turned a lamp on, and the light flickered 3–4 times. The bulb did not work afterwards. My parents were very patriotic and celebratory; holidays were important to them. Yes, bulbs can act funny right before they burn out, but this was different. Also, what a coincidence (which, by now, you might have guessed that I don't believe in): the light flickered and burned out on the 4th of July.

One Christmas morning, my husband and I woke up early and realized the electricity had stopped at some point during the night. I looked over at my clock and it was flashing "12:25." I like to think my parents were saying, "Merry Christmas."

I wish I had a penny (!) for every time our house electricity has gone out since my dad passed. It has happened too many times to count, and the electricity was only momentarily off before it came back on.

While driving one evening around 6:45 PM, I was talking to my husband on my cell phone. He was at home and told me the electricity had gone out. I was thinking about how those on the Other Side can affect electricity, so I jokingly asked my husband what time was flashing on the clock (the particular clock he was looking at flashes the time once the electricity is back on, and the time is not automatically corrected). I was thinking of my dad and the month and day he died (May 26th), and wondering if he had anything to do with the electricity going out. My husband said that the clock was flashing 5:26. It was remarkable!

There are so many times I've looked at the clock and it showed the numbers of either my birthday, one of my parents' birthdays, or one of the days of their passings. For example, my dad was born on

10/4, so when I looked at the clock, it often showed 10:04. Or I was thinking about things before I drifted off to sleep, and for some reason, I looked at the clock and the time showed the numbers of my own birthday, "12:13." Not only that, but several times after the electricity stopped and restarted, I have looked at the clock and "12:13" was flashing. When this happened, I felt my parents were saying "hi" in a very personal way, using my birthday numbers, so I won't have any doubts about who sent me the sign from Heaven. Hello back to you, Mom and Dad! I just love that I don't have to say "goodbye."

Hopeful Hints

- *Do lights, radios or televisions turn on or off on their own? Does this happen around a significant day, such as your birthday or that of a loved one in Heaven, or an anniversary of the passing of a loved one?*
- *Look at odd text messages or numbers displayed on your phone for no apparent reason: What might these odd messages or numbers mean for you?*
- *When you glance at clocks or the time on your phone, do you notice important numbers in your life?*

CHAPTER FIVE

DREAM VISITS

My parents visit me in dreams. I call these gifts: dream visits. Why we are able to connect with our deceased loved ones better when we are sleeping is for more knowledgeable people to explain and is beyond the scope of this book. Here, though, I will mention my most memorable dream visits to date and the profound comfort they've provided me.

I was given one of my most poignant dream visit gifts from my dad not long after he passed five years ago. Crying on my bed, missing my dad, I fell asleep holding my cell phone in my right hand. Once asleep, I had a dream with my dad in it. In this dream, I was sitting alone on a bleacher bench in an empty baseball stadium on a sunny day. My dad—who was thin and young again—walked up the bleacher steps to my right, sat down next to me, took my right hand and held it in his hand. It was very comforting. I immediately woke up.

Upon awakening, and before opening my eyes, I could still feel the heaviness of my dad's hand holding mine. I believed I was still feeling my dad's hand, but upon opening my eyes, I saw I was holding my cell phone! I believe with all my heart that my dad orchestrated this synchronicity so that when he held my hand in the dream visit—it would coincide with my holding my cell phone. He was able to make a gift out of my holding something heavy in my hand, so I could still sense the weight of his hand when I woke up. I'm not that clever to have done this myself; meaning, I know my subconscious did not create this dream. What a comforting dream visit with my dad this was for me at a tearful time of grief.

There were other wonderful, special aspects about this dream visit besides the obvious: my dad consoling me during my sadness. One of the other uplifting parts of this dream visit was how my dad was young, thin, and healthy again. I never knew my dad this way. I've read that those in spirit are often seen—by those who can see them—as young, healthy, and at the physical prime of their earth lives. Another nice part of this dream visit was how my dad, a prior great high school baseball pitcher, who loved baseball throughout his life, staged our visit in a baseball stadium on a sunny day.

Finally, what was remarkable to me about this dream visit was when my dad was walking up the steps to the bleacher where I was, he had his head down, looking at the steps: I knew *anyway* this young, slender man was my dad. This dream was extremely comforting to me, especially because it occurred during a sad time early on in my grief. My dad, of course, knew this would help my heart, which is why the dream visit took place.

Both of my parents appeared in another dream visit at a time when I was reflecting upon what direction to take in my nursing career. In the dream visit, my parents were wearing McDonald's uniforms and hats! I asked my mom, "Mom, do you like your job?" She answered, with the twinkle in her eye my mom was known for, "I'm *lovin'* it!" Now, the thing is, I had this dream either before the McDonald's slogan "I'm lovin' it" came out or before I was aware of it! The dream made me feel my parents were not only with me, but guiding me too. The message, I felt, was to enjoy whatever job I do.

Recently, I dreamed that I was with children in an unknown house. Immediately, I heard my dad's voice behind me, and he was talking to someone I couldn't see. I caught a glimpse of my dad out of the corner of my eye, and he was young, in his 40's, thin, and healthy again! I said to the kids in this dream, "I'm sorry, but I haven't heard my dad's voice in *so* long!" (In the dream, I was aware that my dad had passed) I then turned toward my dad, and all of a sudden, the two of us were in our old living room in the house where I grew up. In the dream at this point, my dad was in his early 60's, healthy as ever in the face, and he had his light blue cardigan sweater on. But again, because I knew he had passed, I was crying so hard, telling him how much I missed him. My dad just listened as he looked at me with compassion.

Here's one of the best parts of this dream visit: I was holding my dad's thumb with my whole hand. Why this was special was because it's similar to what I do when I find a penny: I pretend I'm holding my dad's hand or my mom's hand; sometimes I put the penny between two fingers. I know how odd this sounds, but it's a way I connect with my parents since I know they leave me the pennies (sometimes I find two pennies at the same time, and I hold one penny in each hand). So, I was holding my dad's thumb in this very real dream visit just like how I hold the pennies sometimes in the real world, and I was appreciating that my dad created this clear and wonderful gesture in the dream visit, one he knew would mean so much to me.

The dream I just described was a different type of dream visit. I got to hear the sound of my dad's voice as he spoke many words, although I don't know what the words were. It's the only dream visit with my dad where I've really heard the sound of his healthy voice in a sentence or two. It was wonderful.

In 2008, right before the 23rd anniversary of my mom's passing, I had a dream visit with her. My mom and I were hugging each other very hard and long, and I was crying. In the dream visit, I knew I hadn't seen my mom in so long, and I was telling her how much I missed her. My mom said, "I know" with so much love and compassion. It was consoling beyond words.

I had another dream visit with my mom not too long ago. This dream visit took place when I was hoping to connect with my mom.

In the dream, my mom and my aunt were sitting in a booth at a restaurant, one similar to the restaurant my same aunt and her husband, my uncle, owned and operated. They both looked fantastic! I saw my mom and asked excitedly, "Mom, is that really you?" I knew my mom had passed and it'd been about 25 years since I've seen my Mom alive here on Earth. My mom saw me and stood up, while smiling. We then had the best, longest hug ever. Thank you, Mom. Thank you, God.

Decorating the Christmas tree with my dad will always be one of my most cherished holiday memories. Since he passed, it's been difficult for me to put my dad's ornaments on my Christmas tree during the holiday season. My dad in Heaven knows this, I believe. So, to help me, my dad visited me in a dream. Not only did my dad comfort me during this dream visit, but he also exhibited his wonderful sense of humor. It never ceases to amaze me what they can do simultaneously on the Other Side! My dad also gave me an idea how these dream visits might work, which I'll explain in a moment.

Anyway, in the dream visit on this night in early December, my dad was in his early 60's, healthy, and wearing a colorful shirt. Dad and I were in my current living room in front of my Christmas tree, and we were about to put his ornaments on the tree. (I had not yet felt up for putting my dad's ornaments on my tree in real life.) So, in the dream we were both holding ornaments. I looked at the pretty tree, then at my dad, and said, "But, Dad, we don't have the lights on the tree yet!" My dad looked at me, with a smile on his face and in his eyes, and said dryly, "I forgot about those." I immediately woke up!

My dad was trying to help me do something that was difficult to accomplish without him. He was showing me that he would be there in spirit to help me. When he said, "I forgot about those," he gave me an idea about how dream visits might work. Just from hearing my dad's words "I forgot about those," I began to wonder if our deceased loved ones can "set the stage" in our dream visits, much like the stage and prop directors do in theatre plays. The difference is, I believe, that those in spirit only have to "think" and "will" it, and it happens. Our loved ones are orchestrating the entire setting in the way that they know will comfort us the most. I appreciate your thoughtful, loving gesture, Dad.

Another Christmas-related dream visit happened one night soon after my dad passed. In the dream visit, my sister and I were decorating the Christmas tree at my dad's house, but my dad, who had already passed in the dream, was there too. All of a sudden, my dad was behind my sister in his yellow polo shirt and yellow shorts (in December!). He looked great. In this dream visit, I knew my dad had passed. I said to my sister, "Dad's here! He's right behind you!" I realized I could see him but she could not.

Speaking of my dad doing great, one night before I fell asleep, I asked my dad to help me never see his legs how they were before he passed when he now visited me in my dreams. That night I dreamt about my dad, and I could only see his healthy, nice-looking legs! In the dream described just above, about decorating the Christmas tree with my sister and dad, maybe my dad was wearing yellow shorts in December so he could show me his now good-looking legs!

A few times I have seen my dad in dreams where he did not appear to see me. Perhaps some who know a lot more about these things than I do would say I was "astrally" traveling in my dreams. Astral travel is described as when one's soul travels outside of the physical body. In one of these dreams, my dad was young again. He was working on a carpentry project in a room that didn't have much in it.

Another dream where my dad didn't seem to see me took place before Pope Benedict visited the United States in April of 2008. In the dream, my dad and another person I didn't know were sitting in the stands, waiting to hear someone speak. Next to my dad, I looked down and saw Pope Benedict on the stage. Then I looked at my dad, who didn't see me. When I looked back down at the stage, Pope Benedict was gone, but Pope John Paul II was there instead! I then woke up.

I mentioned one of my best dream visits in my "Potpourri" chapter, where my dad came to me in a dream the night before his first birthday after he passed. I knew he had passed and I was able to tell my dad how much I missed him. He said, "I know." It was so nice. My dad was well too, which was wonderful. As I said earlier, my dad gave me a birthday gift on his birthday!

Another dream I mentioned in the "Best Coins" chapter was one where I was watching my husband and me sleeping. While watching us, I saw a penny drop from Heaven above onto the middle of the end of the bed. A week later, I was emptying my suitcase on the end of the bed. I came back to the suitcase after putting clothes away, and there was penny on my blouse. The location of the penny was right where it dropped onto the bed in my dream a week earlier!

There were common denominators in these dream visits, which helped me know the dreams were orchestrated by my deceased parents and that they really were visiting with me while I slept. One common factor was that each dream visit seemed very real. I remembered all the details vividly then, and still do.

Another common factor was that I woke up right after having the dream visit and just knew I was truly with my mom, dad, or both. This is not similar to the regular dreams I have, where the dream seems distant when I wake up, and I forget about it ten seconds later.

A third common factor I noticed in these dream visits was that my parents didn't move or say much. My guess is that moving and using voice in dream visits require a lot of energy from those who are no longer in a physical body. I would surmise that it is even harder to speak than to appear briefly in a vision. The few times I have heard my deceased parents talk in dream visits, they have only used a few words. And when they appeared briefly in a dream vision, the vision didn't last very long. I feel very fortunate to have received so many dream visits with my parents.

Hopeful Hints

- *When loved ones in Heaven visit us in a dream, it seems very real. Can you still recall vivid details of such a dream? Were your loved ones in Heaven healthy and happy in the dream? These are clues that they indeed visited you.*

- *We often know our loved ones have passed during dream visits with them. Usually, they don't move or talk much, and don't stay long. We wake up right away. Jot down the details (although you may not ever forget them because the dream visit is so real as well as wonderful).*

- *To understand the symbolic message of a dream visit from loved ones in Heaven, consider the following: did you have the dream visit around a special date? Was the setting in the dream significant? What was the activity that took place in the dream?*

CHAPTER SIX

SYNCHRONICITY

As with most of the other signs and gifts I've received, there are too many synchronicity stories to include in this book. Usually the synchronicities involve my thinking or talking about someone or something, and then hearing or reading about the same word, name, or subject matter at the exact same moment.

The following events are just a few examples of the large number of synchronicities I've experienced. I believe God is behind all of these synchronicities, as He is behind everything else! The angels, my parents and other loved ones in Heaven, such as my guides (I now believe we all have our special guides) help make these synchronicities happen.

Given the nature of this book and all of the communication from the Other Side that has led up to it, one of the most astonishing occurrences of synchronicity that has happened involved the word "intuition." One afternoon, while remembering to do it, I decided to change the cartridge on my woman's shaver, called "Intuition." The television was on while I was looking for the new cartridge. Upon finding the new cartridge, I read the name on the package—"Intuition." As I was reading each *syllable* to myself—in * tu * i * tion— I was hearing the very same *syllable* from the word "intuition" on television...at the exact same time!

This synchronicity of events was so incredible to me. It involved not only that specific word (and all that it relates to), but also my hearing each syllable at the exact time I was reading the same syllable. I definitely felt the message for me was along these lines: Everything that is happening and all I've been wondering about is connected to intuition. Intuition can be defined as a form of energetic communication between a person, loved ones (both on Earth and in Heaven), angels and God. It's about perceiving and knowing things that are beyond our rational, deductive, thinking mind. The blunt message for me was this: "It's intuition, Mary—get it?"

Two other incredible synchronicities occurred on the same date, one year apart: April 17, 2007 and April 17, 2008. On April 17, 2007, which was the 22nd anniversary of my mom's passing, I did something I don't typically do (which, as I've said, is how I receive a lot of my signs—doing something out of the ordinary for me). I turned on a rock 'n roll radio station while driving my car, and I heard lyrics about "the day someone dies." I thought, "Hmm…if that was you, Mom, thanks."

Exactly one year later, on April 17, 2008, I was driving in my car again and remembering the radio experience I had had on that same day, 12 months earlier. I thought amusingly to myself, "Maybe I'm supposed to listen to rock radio again!" So I turned on the radio, and I heard the *exact same lyrics,* about "the day someone dies," from the very same song! It was unbelievable! One couldn't replicate this synchronicity even if one tried.

After hearing the same song lyrics again, exactly one year-to-the-day later, on the anniversary of my mom's passing, I laughed, looked up, and said, "That's a good one, Mom and Dad!" I'm comfortable receiving these signs and I am not afraid. If I were fearful, I don't believe I would see the signs. With that said, I would have been more shaken up if this had happened to me five years ago. And if someone else had told me about it, I'm sure I wouldn't have believed the person.

Although I address songs again in a later chapter because they're particularly wonderful gifts from Heaven, as you can tell by the last story, I have to address them here as well. Song-related synchronicities occur when I hear a memorable or important song right when I need to hear it the most—or when those on the Other Side believe I need to hear it!

In the weeks following my dad's passing in May 2004, while driving, I would listen to a CD that was comprised of songs from a DVD I had made for him for his 85th birthday. This was the time period during which I began to become aware of signs from the Other Side. Back then, I began to notice that very often the CD would either end on a particular song or end completely at the exact moment I drove into my garage and parked the car. It happened so often that I couldn't help but notice. Eventually, it seemed to happen every time I played the CD. And it appeared that the outside world was cooperating to help make this happen. I realized that traffic conditions were such that I would have to drive at a certain speed or encounter traffic lights that would have me entering my garage with the song or CD ending at the moment I parked the car. Again, I wouldn't be able to replicate this synchronicity even if I tried.

Not too long after my dad passed, I was on an airplane, and I was thinking about how I had shopped some to distract myself from my grief and sadness. Right then, I turned around and noticed that a woman behind me was holding her newspaper high up in the air. There in large letters were words about how shopping can be therapeutic.

Many times I see license plates with numbers reminding me of people I know or of whom I am thinking. While thinking about my parents when I'm driving, I often see numbers on other car license plates that include the numbers of one of their birthdays or the anniversary date of one of their passings. Or, I'll see one or more cars around me with the numbers of our house address where we lived when I was growing up.

Awhile ago, within a few minutes, I saw four different cars around me while driving with the license plate numbers "526." My dad passed on 5/26.

As I talked about in the chapter on electrical gifts, often I'll happen to look at the clock when it shows a time that is a significant date for me, such as my birthday or one of my parents' birthdays or passings.

Once I found a quarter with the image of a bridge on it. I was about to tell the person I was with about the quarter, but before I could say anything, she said, "I think you have to build a bridge." She was referring metaphorically to something entirely different, having no idea that I had this special coin in my hand.

The next synchronicity event is one that I mentioned earlier in the chapter about coins. It was a moment when I decided to turn on the television one weekend afternoon (something I never do), and the first thing I saw was a penny filling the entire TV screen! I believe that my dad, who communicates with me using pennies, orchestrated the concurrence—where my uncharacteristic desire to watch TV coincided with the significant image showing up on the screen.

Quite some time ago, I was watching television and thinking about starting this book. Right then, a commercial came on and the words spoken were about "one's study," and "letting others help you get started and help you write." I found this amusing because the message could have been from my parents, and they had already helped me with my study by giving me countless signs, many of which have become the material for this book!

As you read in Chapter One, many of my synchronicities involve pennies, and these synchronicities happen often. Too many times to cite here, I will be thinking or talking about pennies and my eyes then see a penny. Frequently, this happens in unusual places, such as outside my car door while waiting at a traffic light.

Also, I couldn't include enough pages in this book to list the countless examples of times when I've thought of a person's name in my head—or have been talking to a person—and then I'll read or hear his or her name at the exact same moment.

When I think about and/or talk to my mom in spirit, I say the word "Mom" in my head. And at the same moment, often, I'll read or hear the word "Mom." Thanks, Mom.

I was writing the chapter about dreams for this book, and when I was about to type the word "exuberantly," I couldn't remember how to spell it. Without trying to, I opened the dictionary to the page that had "exuberantly" as a header!

I have noticed recently that I'll read a word and hear it at the same time much more frequently than before. In fact, the frequency increases greatly when I'm reading a spiritually-oriented book or when I'm writing pages for this book.

As I end this chapter, I want to share one of the most memorable, special, and heartfelt synchronicities that I've experienced, and it happened shortly after my dad passed—well before I'd received so many signs and started believing they were signs of afterlife communication.

I believe very much the following event was a sign orchestrated by both of my parents. One afternoon, I stopped for a salad at a market. Upon returning to my car, I experienced three events within two minutes that left me astounded. First, I noticed my dad facing me—it was a photo of him on the cover of a DVD that was sitting on my passenger seat. Although I couldn't recall doing so, I decided I must have taken this DVD (one made for my dad's 85th birthday) out of the glove compartment when I opened it earlier. Less than one minute after seeing my Dad's picture on a DVD cover, I was reading the newspaper and landed on these words: "Standing by someone in sickness is the greatest expression of love there is." For some reason, right after reading that sentence, I turned over the newspaper to a section I don't normally read, and my eyes went straight to part of a sentence, mid-paragraph, in the middle of the page which said: "Mom and Dad may be close by."

I could not believe it! I felt my parents were with me in spirit right then, and I felt their love.

Hopeful Hints

- *Our loved ones in Heaven often cause us to see or hear their names just when we are thinking about them. Are they letting you know they're with you?*
- *Numbers are big to those in Heaven! Notice how clocks, dates, license plates, and addresses often show numbers significant to you, particularly at special times. Do the numbers reflect something shared by you and your loved ones, such as the address of the old family home? Is the day you notice one of these special numbers an important one?*
- *Those in Heaven can string synchronous events together to send you a message. There are no coincidences. What might be meant by a series of synchronicities?*

CHAPTER SEVEN

GIFTS IN MY HEAD: IMAGES AND WORDS

I have received many brief visions of images and words in my mind. Only twice have I heard words in my head that were not my own; I didn't recognize the voice either time. I will discuss both of these episodes of clairaudience—hearing sounds and words that exist beyond the reach of ordinary experience—as well as significant images that I've received. Some of the images and visions I have seen in my head—which is clairvoyance—have helped me in my grief since my dad passed.

Although I believe everyone has the capacity to receive messages from Heaven in some way if one is open to receiving them, I feel very fortunate to have received these auditory and visual gifts. I do believe they are from God and His messengers, including angels and my parents. Perhaps my parents did not literally create each of the following visions; however, I do believe they "petitioned" on my behalf. I believe this because I never received special images or heard spoken words in my head before my dad passed. I was so sad at that time, and these images and words from Heaven have helped comfort and counsel me.

The majority of the images and visions have occurred in my mind, which is known as my "third eye," by those in the metaphysical world. First, I'll describe an incredible vision that I received with my *opened* eyes. This experience occurred right after I saw Allison DuBois, a well-known and highly regarded medium. The show "Medium" is based on Allison DuBois's life. That night, I stayed at the same hotel where the Allison DuBois event took place. This hotel was filled with all kinds of energy, which I believe was due to the nature of the event, the abilities of this medium, and the quality of experience Allison DuBois created.

After the event, while lying in the hotel room bed, alone in the dark, all of a sudden I was looking at some type of ancient alphabet or script on the ceiling! This unfamiliar script remained visible on the ceiling for several seconds and then the ceiling became dark. I did not recognize the language then, and to this day, I do not know what kind of script it was.

I have no idea why I received this vision, but I do believe it was "easier" for it to occur that night in that hotel due to the intensity of the energy gathered there as a result of an authentic medium's appearance on that particular evening. What was even more remarkable to me than seeing this strange alphabet (or whatever these symbols were on the ceiling of this hotel room) was that I was completely comfortable with seeing it!

Before I describe some of the visions in my head I've had while in an awake state, first I would like to share with you one of the few clairaudient (hearing) experiences I've had (as far as I'm aware of).

Once, while alone at night, in a voice I didn't recognize, I heard the words, "No endings, only beginnings." This occurred one night during the first January after my dad passed, and I was grieving. I believe the message for me to hear was that there are no endings when we pass, only beginnings—and to be assured I was not alone in my grief. What a healing gift this was for me to receive during my days of sadness. Thank you, God, Guardian Angel, Mom and Dad, and anyone else.

During that same January, I saw a vision similar to that of the God of Janus (I had to ask my very smart husband about Greek Mythology to clarify this one, as I don't remember what I learned back in school). The God of Janus is the God of beginnings and endings. The beginning month of the year—January—was named after this Roman God. I received both the above-mentioned auditory message of "No endings, only beginnings," and the vision of the God of Janus during January.

The vision was of an artist's bust (as in a sculpted representation of a person's head and shoulders), but it was different than the God of Janus, which is normally depicted as the same God facing in different directions. In my vision, the left half of the face was a smiling, happy, older teenage boy from the great Roman and Greek era, and his eyes were looking to the left. The right side of the face showed an equally smiling, happy young girl from the Roman and Greek era, and she was looking to the right. In my estimation, the teenage boy was looking towards and representing the past, and the young girl was looking towards and representing the future. This happened shortly after hearing "No endings, only beginnings." I don't know why I received this vision, but I felt protected and not alone.

Another time I saw a brief vision of a golden angel who was leaning to the right, holding a sword in his right hand. There was a small box over his heart and Jesus was in the box! Some might say this was a vision of Archangel Michael, the angel of protection. How beautiful this vision was. The result of seeing this vision was that I began listening again to my Bible CDs. I felt lucky to see this vision—and I needed it too, because I wasn't spending enough time praying to God or Jesus.

In another brief vision in my head, I saw an angel's upper torso "permeate" an entire house. I realize that it might be difficult to totally believe and understand this vision without seeing it yourself as I did. I have never seen any movie or television special effects like it, and furthermore, I don't believe what I saw could be re-created by a special effects team anyway. Every molecule of the angel, or perhaps Jesus, was a part of every atom of the symbolic house in my vision. I believe the house was not a familiar one; it was shown to convey a symbolic message to me that God and angels are integrated with every atom and person here on earth. This vision sure showed me this concept—it was surreal, and very comforting.

Once I had a brief vision of a centaur—the half man and half horse creature of Greek mythology. These Greek-era visions, I believe, are from God and the angels. I'm not a Greek or Latin scholar—I don't remember a lot of basic Latin and mythology I once learned. I had to wonder about my dad's involvement, though, because he *was* a Latin and classical literature scholar. Also, some of these words and visions—such as the message, "No endings, only beginnings," and the centaur—are discussed in books written by one of my dad's favorite Catholic scholars and writers, C.S. Lewis.

I had a brief vision once where I saw my dad, who was much younger in the vision, inside a church and dressed in a monk's robe! I seemed to be a little above my dad and was looking down at him. My dad, the monk, looked very surprised to see me (and if I was astrally traveling, I'll bet he was!).

I attended an event of another famous gifted medium, John Edward. He told me my parents were there at the event (in spirit). Two days after attending John Edward's event, I saw words (in red letters) in my head that said, "We care about you and we're there for you."

Beyond the phenomenal angelic and archetypal images I've received, there has been a variety of other visual gifts. Once, in my head, I saw a burst of light and then I saw either "Loving in Light" or "Love in Light."

During a "Guys & Dolls" musical production, I closed my eyes and saw a heart. At the end of the show, the last stage prop was a big red heart. "Guys & Dolls" was one of my dad's favorite musicals.

Lately, I routinely wake up and see explosions of white clouds (similar to fireworks) followed by a big red heart in my head. How wonderful. Thank you God, angels, guides, and Mom and Dad!

Speaking of fireworks, on the 4th of July one year, I had a vision of fireworks going off, but instead of the sparks going outward, they went inward and formed the shape of a heart.

Twice since my dad passed, and while I was awake, I have seen him in my head as a young man, dressed in overalls, standing outside and surrounded by many sloping, green hills. I felt he was in Ireland. Both times, it was a gorgeous, sunny day and he was standing near a brown fence. These visions were very uplifting and comforting to me, who misses my Irish dad.

Speaking of Ireland, while meditating, and after asking God where my Great-grandfather Shannon was born, I had a vision of the map of Ireland. In the vision, the focus of my attention was directed to a particular bay where there was a red star, similar to one on the Google maps, marking a spot near this inlet. I believe the area was near Donegal, Ireland. After I received this vision, I then remembered how my dad talked about our ancestors living in Donegal County, Ireland. I asked a question about where my great-grandpa was born, and I received the answer in my head via a map of Ireland with a star on it!

After my dad passed, one day I saw the word "shaman" in my head. Although I wasn't clear as to why I saw this powerful word, perhaps the message was confirmation that I'm receiving the help and assistance of a shaman. Or maybe it was a clue that I was a shaman in another life, or that I'm supposed to become one in this life! Who knows.

I found a black and white negative from the 1950's in my dad's photo collection, which showed a man in a hat. I couldn't tell for sure if it was my dad or another man. I asked God, or anyone else "up there," who the man in the hat was in the picture. A day or so later, I had a quick flash of a vision in my mind—it was a black and white image of my dad's smiling face, and he was wearing the hat from the 1950's. My dad was the same man in the photo negative. My request was answered. Thank you, Dad!

The second time I heard words in my head happened once when I was walking to the bathroom in the middle of the night. I heard the words, "You have been chosen as a vehicle of transmission for communication between the two worlds." I don't talk like that when I'm fully awake, much less when I'm sleepy and thinking about getting to the bathroom! This book must be connected to that message.

Another time, I woke up seeing the words "Thank you" in red letters running vertically and to the right of a path that I was seeing on the screen in my head. I later asked who was thanking me and why, and I found a quarter in front of the word "DVD" on a box of DVDs. I believe my parents were thanking me for creating family DVDs. (Of course, I wouldn't have come to this conclusion if the event hadn't happened after finding coins under signs and receiving all of these incredible signs—and answers—from Heaven for over five years)

A pattern is emerging as I write this book. I will complete a chapter, and then my parents or others on the Other Side will give me something else to add to the chapter! I love it. In this case, I believe they wanted to "mix things up" a bit.

After completing this chapter, I had a brief vision of the outline of a cat! The lines making up this cat outline were comprised of *moving light*—that's the best way I can describe it. The lines weren't made of fire, but they weren't similar to electrical light from light bulbs either. Yes, the cat outline was moving light. Here's the best part: It didn't look like a normal cat, but I intuitively knew it was my old cat, Richard, whom we had to put down many years ago. I immediately said, "Richard!" The first feeling I had was one of surprise, and then I thought about how nice it was that he came to visit. And then I realized how strange it was that I knew it was my cat, Richard, even though this outline didn't look a thing like him.

Not long ago, I was wondering about a ring I found (discussed in an earlier chapter). This was the ring with an ancient design that looked to be either Egyptian or Native American. I had been thinking that it was probably a Native American design, but upon finishing the first draft of this chapter, I had two brief visions of ancient Egyptian statues, which somehow made me think the ring showed an Egyptian design after all.

I saw a brief vision in my head that showed three or four royal blue, vertical columns. It seemed that the columns came to a triangular peak at the top. Although these other-worldly objects and their meaning are still a mystery to me, I found them comforting.

I woke up abruptly one morning and saw approximately four vertical streams of white mist. The streams were about four inches long, and they were moving up, away from me and toward the ceiling! I closed and reopened my eyes, and these mist-like appearances were still there. I wasn't afraid. I felt I was being given a new type of sign, and I like to think it was angelic in nature. All I know is that I'm glad this mist experience happened quite some time after I had received a lot of other signs, because I do believe I would've been totally freaked out at an earlier time!

Another sign happened not long after finishing and reviewing this chapter and hopeful hints. I sent an e-mail with the below hopeful hints, and received a return e-mail with my original e-mail written entirely in Greek, except for the below hints! Even the part from AOL that shows when the e-mail was sent and from whom—all of it was written in Greek. I couldn't have put it in Greek, even if I had tried. I called my e-mail recipient and asked her if the e-mail showed Greek on her end, and she said it didn't!

The bottom line is this: I wrote about Greek images in this chapter, titled: "Gifts in My Head: Images and Words." I then received an e-mail of mine returned back to me with all of my hopeful hints surrounded by Greek words! I think they in Heaven want me to be aware of and practice the hints that I preach!

I am adding to this chapter once again, toward the completion of writing this book. Recently, while waking up, I had a quick vision of my dad. He said "I do the best I can." I then saw the red heart in my head that I often see while waking up. I love receiving this gift and all of the others, as long as I'm not keeping my dad or taxing him. I have told both my parents many times of my gratitude and concern as well. But, I still receive the signs, so I believe I'm supposed to, for now.

As I close this chapter, I'll share about the time I saw a bridge in my head, followed by the word "peace." This reminded me of a beautiful saying I once saw in my inner vision while falling asleep, "Go in peace and peace will follow."

Hopeful Hints

- Be aware of unusual images in your mind unrelated to what you are thinking about at the moment. Perhaps you are being given a symbolic message in pictures. How does the symbolic message connect to what is going on in your life?

- Keep a pad of paper and pen near your bed and write down any words or images you hear or see in your head upon awakening (or drifting off to sleep). What message might be contained in these images and words?

- When you're thinking of a loved one who has passed, especially with great emotion, notice whether any recurring images or words accompany those strong feelings. What comforting message do you imagine you might be receiving?

CHAPTER EIGHT

SPECIAL SONGS

Since my dad passed in 2004, I often hear songs playing in my head as I am waking up. The music is usually in the background, similar to how radio music can be. The songs and lyrics I hear are significant to me. Many songs are special ones from the old musicals my parents, siblings, and I enjoyed listening to many years ago (and even now). I believe my parents, and especially my dad, have something to do with my hearing music as I wake up, because I never heard songs in my head before my dad passed.

Not only have I awakened to songs playing in my head, but I believe I've received specific communication from my parents in this way. There is much information written about how those who have passed will use songs or music as a way to communicate with loved ones on earth; perhaps one of the reasons is because it is an easier energetic method for them to convey messages.

One of my most stunning—and unbelievable, if it hadn't happened to me—song gifts is the one that I detailed in Chapter Six on synchronicities. It was the experience of hearing lyrics about "the day someone dies" on the anniversary of my mom's passing two years in a row.

This song gift is a good example of my parents' humor—and they each had such a wonderful sense of humor. As I keep saying, I really *love* seeing the continual display of their humor, wit and fun in the signs they send because it's evidence to me: Mom and Dad are doing just *great* in Heaven.

Another humorous song gift came from my dad on Halloween last year. I woke up on Halloween morning with the song "Ain't Misbehavin," written by Fats Waller and sung by Louis Armstrong playing in my head. There are a couple reasons why "Ain't Misbehavin" playing on Halloween is significant. As I described, my dad was Irish, Catholic, religious, humorous, and very much appreciated and celebrated the holidays, including Halloween (or the Eve of the Souls). As you may know, Halloween involves the souls being mischievous on Halloween, the eve of All Saints Day—and I'm hearing "Ain't Misbehavin" on this particular morning. I loved it.

However, this Halloween event is even more significant and personal for the following reason. For my dad's 85th birthday, I created a video with photos from all periods of his life. One of the songs I sang to accompany the pictures from one of the earlier decades of my dad's life was "Ain't Misbehavin," written by Fats Waller and sung by Louis Armstrong. After hearing this song in my head on Halloween morning, I thanked my dad and God.

The experience brought back the feeling of how my dad was so full of spirit and tradition on the holidays, including Halloween. Really, though, my dad was full of spirit and tradition all the time. I cannot adequately express the wonderful and comforting feelings this sign and gift bring to me.

Speaking of Halloween-related phenomena, another song incident involved our black cat, Eamon. (Eamon, by the way, was named by my dad while he was here, after an Irish Prime Minister from the early 1900's—Eamon de Valera) As I shared earlier, I am convinced that our cat, Eamon, was sent to us by my mom and my Aunt Kathleen, who are both in Heaven. The reasons I believe Eamon was sent to us are many. Both Aunt Kathleen and our family had black cats (who were related). I am a huge cat lover. Cats provide me much joy and comfort.

Anyway, since we adopted Eamon—which was at a time when my dad's health was declining—I began singing a song with one word in it: Eamon. I sing it to the tune of the TV show *Jeopardy* after I sweep Eamon off his paws. While I'm holding him, I talk to him, telling him that I *know* his grandma and his great-Aunt Kathy sent him to me. I've been talking and singing to Eamon in this way for years now: thanking my mom and Aunt Kathleen in between verses, while singing the Eamon song to *Jeopardy* music!

So, in July of 2007, I was at an event at which the famous psychic-medium, John Edward, gave numerous readings to many grateful audience members. At one point, John Edward said, "I'm hearing the *Jeopardy* song." I didn't put my hand up quickly because John Edward had already spoken with me (I talk about this later, in another chapter), and he was swiftly pulled in another direction. But, I *know* my mom and dad put this *Jeopardy* song in John Edward's head, knowing I would make the connection. Mom and Dad knew I'd realize the song was for me from them.

By putting the *Jeopardy* song in John Edward's head, my parents showed their awareness. They are aware that I attribute the gift of Eamon as being one from my mom and my Aunt Kathleen. They hear me thanking them for Eamon. And they are with me when I sing the Eamon song to the *Jeopardy* melody. How nice. What a gift.

Often I wake up hearing songs of love playing in my head. The music is playing in the background (in my head) as I am thinking about something totally unrelated. The songs are ones I know and are often ones I selected to use in videos created for family members.

I know my parents are behind my hearing songs that hold meaning for me. As I've mentioned before in another chapter, occasionally I've heard my parents say a few words in a dream visit, but not often. I believe it must be easier and takes less energy for our loved ones in Heaven to communicate through songs. I imagine all they have to do is press a button on the jukebox!

Here is another example of how a song and synchronicity occurred together for me (the other big example was the one on the anniversary of my mom's passing). When I was driving somewhere once and thinking about how my mom always beamed when she smiled, a song came on the radio right then, and I heard lyrics about someone beaming while smiling!

On different nights I have awakened while singing verses sung at the Catholic Mass—"Alleluia" and "Glory to God in the Highest and Peace to His People on Earth." I'm not entirely sure why I woke up singing these verses, but I appreciate the beautiful religious words and music. Thank you, God.

These are just a few of the ways music and songs were utilized by my parents, God, and others to let me know they were nearby. As with the other types of gifts, I can't cite each and every song sign I've received—especially all the synchronistic experiences connected with songs. But the ones I've shared are those that have given me the most joy and comfort.

Hopeful Hints

- *Loved ones in Heaven can project music and/or song lyrics in your head, especially as you are waking up or falling asleep. These sounds may resemble background music when you are relaxing and thinking about something else. Keep pen and paper handy near your bed so you can write down songs as you hear them.*

- *Do you hear a familiar tune but no lyrics as you wake up or fall asleep? Make note of the song title so you can look up the lyrics later. Do the lyrics ring true? Why did your loved one play that particular song?*

- *Is the music in your head significant to the date or season? If you hear "Jingle Bells" around Christmas, for example, was "Jingle Bells" your father's favorite Christmas carol?*

CHAPTER NINE

UNDER SIGNS AND WORDS

The best examples of coins and other gifts I've found under signs or words are included here. I described times I found cheese crackers under words in another chapter, so I won't mention those again.

One of the most touching coin-in-front-of-a-sign events happened while I was at Safeway one day. There, at the end of an aisle, was a large display of "Healthy Pop" popcorn by the company named "Jolly Time." Positioned nowhere near a cash register in front of one of these "Healthy Pop" boxes—was a penny. My dad—or "pop"—was telling me that he's "healthy" now and having a "jolly" time! This message was given to me early on after my dad passed and it made me feel so good.

While on vacation last summer, months after finishing this chapter, I asked for the second time if I was on the right track in writing this book. Earlier, I described how I found a penny in front of cheese crackers after the first time I asked God, angels, Mom, Dad, and anyone else in Heaven this question. So, after asking a second time, I found a penny in front of our hotel. One minute after that, a cheese cracker was in my path—and not just a regular cheese cracker, but a tan-colored cheese cracker! Of course it was tan—we were at the beach! I appreciated my parents' lightheartedness and I laughed.

Speaking of receiving confirmation about whether or not I should be writing this book, I found a penny under a sign at the fabric store, and the words on the sign were "Express Yourself."

Another coin-under-words incident occurred while in Tahoe City. While walking out of restaurant, I saw a dime on the ground right under an outdoor valet parking podium on which an opened book was placed. And the book was opened to pages with all kinds of information about electromagnetic energy on them! This incident reminded me of the Pokemon card I once found that I wrote about in an earlier chapter, the one that had the word "Energy" on it.

I have wondered many times about how those on the Other Side are able to give us on Earth all of these signs. I was having this thought again after my uncle's funeral while walking in his hometown of Norwood. I looked up and saw a sign that said "Norwood Energy." Another time I found a penny near a can with the word "Voltage" written on it.

In my ongoing inquiry about how our loved ones in Heaven make physical items such as pennies appear, I recall two other times when I received quick replies. One time was when I was at Staples office supply store and came across a penny under a sign that said "Easy." The other time, I found a coin under a box that said "Magic."

On that same beach vacation I mentioned earlier, I found a 1964 penny in front of Jolly Rancher candy. My younger sister and I used to buy Jolly Rancher candy all the time when we were at the beach in the 1960's.

On the anniversary of my mom's passing this past year, I found a penny under a store sign that said "Discovery Too." Five minutes later, I found "two" ("too") pennies lying next to each other in a Barnes & Noble store lobby. I had "discovered" the "two" pennies! Apparently, at this point my parents or others were taking things to a new level…sending me on a scavenger hunt!

In the middle of the Macy's store there was a dime under the

"Prescriptives" make-up counter. Finding coins from the Other Side has been a successful "prescription" for my grief since my dad passed.

Another time I found a penny near a small sign in Borders bookstore that said, "I've shared the joy of reading." This was definitely a message from both my mom and dad, as they instilled the love of reading into all of us kids.

I have found coins near a Title company, a Realty company, and near sidewalk dispenser boxes that hold free real estate magazines many times. My mom became a real estate broker and sold real estate later in her life, after raising 7 kids. She was, just for the record, not only very nice and popular (she was the 1938 May Queen at the University of Nebraska, as I mentioned earlier), but she was extremely bright, like my dad. She graduated with a B.A. degree in Business Education with honors, at a time when only 11% of women graduated from college. My mom was a teacher before entering the U.S. Navy as a W.A.V.E. at the start of WW II. While serving our country, my mom reached the U.S. Naval officer rank of Lt. j.g. My dad, by the way, served as Lt. Commander. I have wonderful memories of my mom when I was young. She was so nice, loving and I could trust her with all my heart. You can see why I'm so proud of my mom and feel so lucky that she was my mother. I am equally proud and feel just as lucky to have had my dad as my father as well. I will now continue sharing my gifts from my parents.

In Chapter Seven, I wrote about the image I saw upon waking up one morning in June of 2008: the words "Thank You" laid out on a path (in my mind). I asked anyone in Heaven to identify who was saying "thank you" and why. I later found a quarter in front of a sign at Safeway that said "DVD." I had recently completed two family DVDs to give to my two nieces as wedding gifts. These DVDs included lots of pictures of my parents, my nieces' grandparents.

I wanted to give them something special to pass down, especially because it showed pictures of their grandparents sharing moments with them when they were small. My mom passed before her oldest grandchild was five years old. Her oldest grandchild was one of my two nieces (these nieces are sisters) who were getting married. So, I felt it was my mother thanking me for making the DVDs.

By the way, during readings with two separate mediums—one of whom was world-renowned, gifted medium, George Anderson—each one independently told me that my mother was showing them colors. Both mediums said that when those on the Other Side show colors, they are referring to creativity. I told both mediums that I had been making family DVDs, and each medium said it was the making of the DVDs to which my mom was referring.

More recently, I found a dime under the DVD section at Safeway that had a big DVD sign above it. Again, this dime was nowhere near the cash registers.

Bookstores are always great places to find signs from Heaven. I told the story about how I was inexplicably drawn toward a chair at Barnes & Noble one day, and I found the magazine insert that said, "Live to the Edge of Your Imagination." I most definitely am.

Well, on another day, I was all ready to purchase a few psychic books for someone else, including two great ones, *Hello from Heaven* by Bill Guggenheim and Judy Guggenheim and *Embraced by the Light*, by Betty J. Eadie. I received a cell phone call while in the bookstore, so I headed toward the door, temporarily placing my books on a shelf on my way out. After completing the call, I came back inside but I couldn't remember where I had put the books. I must have spent 10 minutes looking for them. And right when I was ready to give up, I found them. There, in front of a book about the universe called *Cosmos* by Carl Sagan, I found *Hello from Heaven* and *Embraced by the Light*. Nice one.

My husband and I were about to walk into a California Pizza Kitchen restaurant for a meal when I found a penny in front of the restaurant. I grew up in California, and we had so many special gatherings in our own California Kitchen.

I was on an escalator in an in-door shopping mall when I looked to my left at the enormous windows of the Borders bookstore. My eyes spotted a penny on the rug inside one of the huge windows. Above the penny, there was a very large poster by the London Company called "Paper Chase," and on it was a big purple wax seal with a large fingerprint in it. Underneath this fingerprint—or calling card, if you will—were the words "With Love." As usual, my dad and mom were able to deliver more than one message with this event: They showed me that they can put pennies in the most unreachable places. They ID'd themselves by leaving a fingerprint! Most importantly, though, they expressed their love in a dramatic way. I loved it—and you both, Mom and Dad!

There is even more significance to this penny-fingerprint–wax seal event that I'll describe in a later chapter called "The Fingerprint Penny."

This next wonderful gift occurred not too long ago. A Mass of Intention for my parents was scheduled to be said at our Catholic church one Saturday afternoon. Earlier in the day, I was at Macy's and came across a Lenox box with a large picture of a bouquet of white roses with a cross on top of the roses. In front of this box was a penny!

White roses symbolize remembrance, represent Heavenliness, and are an expression of spiritual love and respect. I had already found 50 million pennies (a slight exaggeration) over the last five years, and the medium, George Anderson, confirmed (without any hints from me) that my parents give me pennies and dimes. So on this day, I found a penny in front of this box with spiritual symbols on it—and less than an hour before a Mass was said in honor of my parents. Also, whenever I light candles in church for my individual family members in spirit, I find a penny within minutes upon leaving the church. These events alone should convince skeptics. But if not, I have many more signs and gifts to share!

I found both a nickel and a penny directly underneath a new calendar for customers to buy in Kinko's (nowhere near the cash register). The calendar showed a red-haired girl at the beach, and showed these words "...from the Heart of the Home." Also—this is the best part—the coins were approximately ten inches directly below this phrase on the calendar: "Trying to arrange my life so I don't even have to be present." Because I know they in Heaven are full of joy and good humor, I laughed when I read this phrase above these coins! (If I believed someone *alive* here on earth sent me a message such as this one, I might have interpreted it in a different way).

Now, I still laugh reading that phrase above because, after finding coins, gifts, and after receiving evidence of various types of communication from my parents for five years, I know without a doubt the coins were placed under this calendar by my dad, or both my mom and dad, and they knew I would laugh. It made me laugh like all of these signs did: the tan cracker at the beach, the coin in front of the cardboard family, and the cheese cracker next to the crystal animals at the Swarovski store. This is my parents' humor. Period.

In closing, I'll mention that it is always soothing to find coins under rainbows, balloons and/or flowers. It is not a coincidence. When this happens to you, someone in Heaven is sending you love!

Hopeful Hints

- *Ask a question of, or request a sign from, your loved one in Heaven. Notice when and where you receive your next sign from Heaven: It may be your answer.*
- *Notice the location of your sign. Is your sign underneath or next to something with words on it? Ponder the meaning: Are the written words near your sign from Heaven for you too?*
- *Do you observe more than one sign from Heaven at the same time?*

CHAPTER TEN

BIRDS AND FEATHERS

Many people report seeing birds and feathers—butterflies too—as signs of afterlife communication from loved ones in Heaven. I have mentioned a few of my butterfly signs earlier, and have collected even more over time.

I have found feathers and bird signs in my path over the last several years. It is my belief, after everything I've experienced and learned since my dad passed 5 years ago, that these bird and feather signs are gifts from my spirit guide, as well as from my parents.

By the way, this is as good a place as any to mention this side note. I do believe one way our loved ones in Heaven can help us heal is by giving us pets. I believe our loved ones can whisper into our loving pets' ears, too. Now, I'll return to my story about bird and feather signs.

Too many times to count, I have found feathers in my path. Sometimes I find them in the most unusual locations (on a church bench) or at an unexpected time (while in church!). I will not cite all my feather signs here except for the one incident described below. But, before I do, I want to thank my guides, loved ones in Heaven, and God for the caring and love sent with each feather, as well as with all of my gifts sent from Heaven.

The most incredible feather event-sign happened when I found a beautiful large feather in my path once. I put it in my car trunk, and then went into a store. Upon returning to my car minutes later, I found this same feather *outside* my car on the asphalt! I do not know why this happened. My guess is to get my attention. And it did!

Some people say that they see various types of birds, such as cardinals, blue jays, doves, hawks, and eagles, for example, as signs from Heaven. The bird signs I've received (of which I am aware) are mostly referencing the eagle. The dove is the other type of bird I've seen often, and I do believe it is a sign from Heaven. Many times I've seen a dove outside our window looking in my direction for the longest time. But the eagle is the bird I see most often in my bird signs. Here are a few of my favorite eagle signs.

It has been since May 2008 that I have noticed eagles, or references to them. I already mentioned in an earlier chapter how I found an eagle medallion next to me at the Truckee River in Tahoe City, California. A week after finding this medallion, I had a brief vision (in my mind) of an eagle's head. A few days later, I had a quick flash of a golden wing while thinking about other things. Finally, just a couple of days after the golden wing vision, I received address labels with the same eagle head I saw in my vision one week earlier!

It was almost dark outside as I was walked along the asphalt when I saw a penny-sized object on the ground, illuminated by the parking lot light. Thinking it was another penny-gift, I picked it up, but discovered it was a small round disk with an eagle on it. It read "Gleneagles," and there was an eagle picture on it. I found out later this disk was representative of the Gleneagles Golf Resort in Scotland. I like to think it was a sign from my Irish, golf-loving dad in spirit. Maybe he'd been playing at Gleneagles Golf Resort in Scotland, and left a souvenir here to let us know.

Here are other times I have received signs relating to eagles. In an earlier chapter, I mentioned I found the ring around the same time I was finding feathers in unusual locations. Sometimes I have found pennies under eagle signs or pictures, such as when I found a 1976 penny under a Dakota Watch Company sign with an eagle on it. Another time I found a penny right behind a car with an eagle sticker on it. One of my favorite eagle signs, though, was when I found an eagle picture under the word "Imagination."

Awhile ago, the following five events occurred on the same day. First, I was talking to someone who had an eagle on his shirt. Later that day, I was driving behind a motorcyclist with an eagle on the back of his jacket. Moments after that, right after finally realizing the word "eagle" was in a song I listen to often, a truck drove by with "Screamin' Eagle" written on it. On this day of eagle signs, I noticed, really for the first time, the eagle on our mailbox! And finally, I think some of my orb (spirit) pictures show eagles (but that's for another book!).

In summary, I have had many bird and feather signs—too many for me not to notice.

Hopeful Hints

- *Repetition of signs can send a message and let us know we aren't alone: If you notice such repetition, consider what the reason might be.*
- *Feathers, coins, butterflies, birds, and particulars scents are among the many signs your loved ones may choose to send. Often there is one main sign. Why did your loved one choose it?*
- *You may receive different signs involving the same theme. Do you see a pattern to your various signs?*

CHAPTER ELEVEN

JOHN EDWARD—MEDIUM

In early 2007, after receiving tickets to see the famous gifted medium, John Edward, on March 11th in New York City, I discovered John Edward scheduled an event for July 14th in Washington DC (near my home). So, I decided to attend that event as well, as I've read all books written by John Edward. Although I've referred to these two extraordinary events at various points in this book, there is much more that happened. I will explain.

Several nights leading up to the first event in New York, scheduled for March 11th, I would wake up at 3:11 AM. I also woke up several times at 12:13 AM—my birthday is December 13th.

Two nights before the first John Edward event in March of 2007, I had a very vivid dream. In the dream, I was with my sister, and we were at a John Edward event! Also in this dream, I needed to excuse myself to use the ladies' room, and while in there, a girl came in and told me that "Joe" came through for me. My dad was known as "Joe" when he was young, as I've mentioned, by relatives and friends in Boston throughout his life. In the dream, I went back to my seat, looked up and saw that John Edward was looking down at me. He said, "Joe came through, but he said he'd come back another time." I responded (in the dream), saying, "That's okay, because I have tickets for another event." John Edward then said, "That's a good one," (which is what my husband often says when I tell him about a sign from Heaven). I woke up, looked at the clock, and again, the clock showed the numbers of the date I was going to see John Edward: 3:11.

During the *actual* John Edward event in New York on March 11th, John Edward did say, "I have Joe here," but another spirit came through for him right away. It all happened so fast that I didn't immediately make the connection between my dad being the "Joe" John Edward was referring to and my prophetic dream in which John Edward told me "Joe" came through.

Later on during the actual event, I did raise my hand, even though someone else was standing up right next to me. When John Edward said, "He let you know he would be here today," my hand just shot up, as I remembered my prophetic dream from two nights earlier. But just as quickly as my hand went up, it came down, because someone raised her hand and John Edward called on her.

I did not receive a reading that night, just as I didn't in my dream (which is why I had the dream, I've decided—my dad was letting me know ahead of time). In my earlier prophetic dream, according to John Edward, "Joe" said he'd come back another time. And I still had another ticket to see John Edward in July!

The night before the July 14th John Edward event in Washington DC, I dreamt again I was at yet another John Edward event! In the dream, I was waiting for the event to start. I looked up, and John Edward was just looking at me—only this time he didn't say anything.

The next morning, I immediately looked at the clock upon awakening and it showed the exact numbers of the day's date— "7:14"—just like the clock had read the morning of the day I saw John Edward on March 11th—"3:11."

After the multiple dreams and clock incidents, I was not going to be surprised if something unusual happened at the John Edward event that evening. Later on, at the event, John Edward was talking to people sitting right next to me. After awhile, John Edward asked, "The woman next to you, has your mom passed?" A woman in front of me asked, "Me?" John Edward responded, "No, the woman there"—pointing at me. I answered, "Yes." John Edward immediately said, "She's here, your mom's here." Then, he quickly asked, "Who's the congestive heart failure connection?" I replied, "My dad." John

Edward quickly asked, "Passed?" I answered, "Yes." John Edward then said, "Your parents are here." All of this transpired within seconds. Thank you, John Edward, for this acknowledgment from my parents. And thank you, Mom and Dad, for validation of your loving presence at John Edward's events.

Two mornings after this second—very real—John Edward event, I woke up and saw words written in red letters in my head. My first thoughts were, "I have words in my head. I think I'll read them." Then, before I realized what the words were, I said to myself, "Oh, they rhyme." And finally, I comprehended the words. The words in my head, two mornings after John Edward's event, were: *"We care about you and were there for you."*

Mom and Dad, thank you for coordinating all of these dreams, clock, and John Edward events. Thank you for your presence.

Hopeful Hints

- *If you ever plan to attend a medium's event, consider writing down what happens to you before the event, both while awake and during your dreams. Are you being given a message?*
- *Should anyone ever offer you tickets to see a medium at the last minute, try to accept and go: you were meant to be at the event! Perhaps you'll learn or receive a reading yourself.*
- *After the event, write down what a medium says about your loved ones as soon as possible so you won't forget.*

CHAPTER TWELVE

GEORGE ANDERSON—MEDIUM

After attending the public events with the medium, John Edward, in 2007, I decided to receive an in-person, one-on-one reading with George Anderson, another world-renowned gifted medium. I had read all the books written by and about George Anderson, as well as the ones by John Edward.

One day in early December of 2007, I was using a calculator while thinking about my upcoming reading with George Anderson, scheduled to take place on my birthday, December 13th. At that moment, I looked down at my calculator and the numbers displayed were "12133." My appointment was scheduled to take place on 12/13 at 3:00 PM.

The day before the reading, on December 12, 2007, I took the train to New York from Baltimore. Similarly to what happened when I was on my way to John Edward's events, or when I was traveling to my dad's family reunion, I received a lot of signs on my way to meet George Anderson. So many signs happened that it made me think my parents were excited they'd be able to communicate with me even better with the help of a gifted medium in a one-hour private reading. The reason I say this is because I began finding coins from the get-go after arriving at the train station. Also, I *felt* my dad was with me.

All four of these next described penny incidents happened within about 5-6 minutes. I bought my train ticket and there was a penny on the floor to my right on the floor. I sat down, decided to buy a newspaper from the outside stand, and there were two 2001 pennies by the stand. I was with my dad in San Jose, California on

9/11/2001. I believe my dad put the two 2001 pennies together as his way of acknowledging I was traveling to New York. Then, I sat down to read and saw another penny near the ticket counter that I didn't see before (which I don't believe was there earlier). So, I had 4 pennies in my hand and I hadn't even boarded the train.

At Penn Station, where we stopped before transferring to another train, I found two dimes and one penny in the line at Starbucks, and another penny leaving a store in the train station. At this time, I now had six pennies and two dimes.

While sitting on the train, on my way to my final destination, my eyes came across something ahead of me on the floor of the train, centered between those eight passengers who sit across from each other—four on each side. There, right in the middle of the floor between these eight passengers—was a penny! I had not yet arrived in New York, and I now had seven pennies, two dimes—and, as I've mentioned before, there were seven kids and two parents in my immediate family.

At the start of my reading with George Anderson, he said, "I have a male energy who states he is Dad and he has Mom with him." I cannot express how comforting it was to hear these words from George Anderson. My mom passed over 24 years ago, and to hear that she was with my dad was indescribable. It was the first thing my dad said to George—my dad knew what I'd love to hear more than anything: Mom and Dad are together again after being apart for over 19 years, since my mom passed in 1985. What wonderful and joyful news to hear.

George Anderson said that the room was full (of spirits). My parents received the longest time to talk via George, the medium. This, of course, was what I wanted and needed. To connect with my mom after so many years was, well, heaven! I really felt my parents were there with me, and that they were both healthy in the spirit world. What proved this for me more than anything was how their personalities came through! My dad was feisty here on Earth, for example, especially when he was healthy, so I loved hearing his feistiness during this reading because it showed me my dad was doing great.

At one point toward the end of the hour, in fact, George Anderson was mentioning something, when he stopped and exclaimed, "My, your dad can be impatient sometimes! He's busting my chops, saying 'She knows what's going on!'" I cracked up! It definitely sounded just like my dad when he was healthy. I believe that anyone who really knew my dad when he was healthy would agree that this sounds just like him. (I also think that my dad became impatient, if you will, with George because the hour was just about up and George was talking about something that, maybe, just wasn't important to my dad!)

Others besides my parents in the spirit world were given time to communicate. I've read that spirits can gain strength from one another in a group. I don't know if this is true, of course, but it would help explain how the spirits were able to stay for an hour. I also believe that respect, generosity, and graciousness exist in Heaven in large amounts—and spirits allowed others to have their turn to communicate through the medium. Also, George Anderson is very sensitive and wanted to acknowledge all of those in spirit who were present with that same kind of respect.

One of the most precious moments of the reading occurred at the end when George Anderson told me the spirits were pulling back their energy and indicated they had to go soon. So, thinking about the many coins I'd received over the past few years, I asked: "Mom, Dad, could you please put an image in George's head what I think you've been doing?" I could have been referring to anything—the dream visits, lights flickering, pictures falling over, synchronicities—all of which have happened in abundance. I didn't say, "Could you put an image of those little round brown things from Heaven I think you've been dropping?" I had not given George Anderson any information, by the way, about finding coins.

George Anderson responded, saying, "Okay. They're showing me signs. *Coins!* Your dad's giving me the A-Okay sign and I'm seeing pennies and dimes."

I wasn't surprised at all. I already knew. Who else would have given me so many coins, so often, for so long—and particularly during special events that were associated with my parents? No one else—just Mom and Dad. (Well, apparently the Angels and my guides help out with the "silver" coins, but that's another story...)

So the incredible reading had come to an end, and not only was it a very validating, healing experience, thanks in large part to this gifted medium, George Anderson, but it was also one of the best birthday presents ever from my parents! Thank you, Mom and Dad!

Hopeful Hints

- *Our loved ones in Heaven give us clues they are nearby. Do you sometimes feel as you did when you were with your loved one here on earth? Do you just know your loved one in Heaven is around, though you can't "prove" it?*
- *Research mediums and obtain references before talking to one. There are many authentic, credible, gifted mediums as well as less capable ones.*
- *Should you ever have a reading with an authentic medium, an indication your loved one is indeed coming through is the emotion you experience as the medium speaks: Do you feel your loved one is in the room, regardless of the medium's exact words? If so, your loved one most likely is with you.*

CHAPTER THIRTEEN

MARACAS

One day, I spoke to a psychic medium by phone, and she asked me if my dad played a musical instrument. The medium said my dad was appearing to her holding both hands up and was shaking them, as if he was playing a pair of maracas. I replied, "No," and told her he didn't play a musical instrument. However, I did share with this medium that my dad used to shake peanuts in his hand before eating them.

About an hour after talking with this medium, I made the real connection! When I find pennies, I am so elated that I put my hands up and shake them! My dad was showing the medium that he sees me and is with me when I'm full of joy after finding pennies and other gifts from him! How wonderful it felt to make this connection, with the medium's help. My dad is truly with me, seeing me, and sharing in my happiness as I celebrate his gifts from Heaven.

A half hour after making this connection, I was in the checkout line at Safeway when I spotted a penny on the floor several feet away (and not in the checkout line). I knew that this penny hadn't been there five minutes earlier, because I had walked through the same section. When I saw the penny, I put my hands up, shook my car keys and said, "Yes!" I realized then that I was shaking my car keys just as someone would shake maracas!

Thank you, Dad, for letting me know in this particular way that you are with me when I feel such joy after finding your pennies and gifts from Heaven.

Hopeful Hints

- *To receive signs, you don't have to talk to a medium. Consider how you feel when you find a sign? Are you happy and full of joy? Do you feel different than normal? You very well may be sensing your loved one right at that moment.*

- *Be aware of your circumstances when you experience signs from Heaven, as you may receive a second sign referencing your first sign. You may dream, for example, of finding a penny next to the refrigerator, and your mom (who has passed) is by your side in this dream. Later, awake, you find a penny next to a refrigerator. Your mom gave you a clue she would be there when you found the penny, and she is!*

- *It takes energy for those in spirit to communicate with us. Remember to thank them for their loving gifts from Heaven!*

CHAPTER FOURTEEN

KEYS

I have found various types of keys—diary, door, paper—in my path many times over the last 5 years. Keys, as you know, symbolize unlocking, opening, and/or discovering things, such as diaries, doors, dreams, valuables, and even hearts.

Here are a few of my memorable gifts involving keys. One night, after my husband and I arrived home about the same time in separate cars, I heard a clunky kind of noise coming from the back of my car. Being tired, I actually forgot about it until the next morning when I tried to drive out of garage. I called a mechanic after discovering the flat tire, and as he was changing the tire, I asked him if it was caused by a nail. Looking at the tire myself, I could see that a piece of gold was totally imbedded in the tire. I retrieved my husband's pliers, pulled it out, and discovered that it was a long, uncut gold key! The mechanic said he'd been working on cars for 23 years and had never seen a key in a tire. This uncut gold key wasn't very sharp and had gone into the tire at a perfect perpendicular angle.

I'm not sure when it happened, but my ability to drive home the previous night hadn't been affected at all. Everything was completely normal until I arrived home. (By the way, we don't have uncut gold keys lying around our property!)

I called my husband and told him about the gold key. This event happened after years of receiving signs from Heaven, so I said, "Honey, this is a sign from heaven. I don't know what it means yet, but it's a sign." A minute later, after saying goodbye to my husband, I went back to look at the key. I just about fell over when I saw "ESP" written on the gold, uncut key! (ESP is the key brand name)

As someone who's received so many signs, I believe signs are symbolic, especially signs involving keys. My husband and I reflected on the message behind this key sign. Neither my husband nor I are 100% sure what the message is, but we came up with some ideas.

The message could be a literal statement of what happened: "You are home with the key of ESP rooted in the wheel that drives you. Release the key, shape it, and move forward as you unlock doors."

The key was embedded in my tire, or wheel. This could be symbolically related to either shamanism (as I mentioned in a previous chapter, I once saw the word "shaman" in my head) and/or chakras (body energy centers): Wheels are an important part of both shamanism and chakras.

Months after receiving this uncut, gold key in my tire (!) in my garage, I had another key-related event involving my car in our garage.

One night, I had a dream where I saw a face on the floor of my car, near my left foot, and it was talking to me! In the dream, my car was parked in the garage, and I was sitting inside the car. I didn't like this smiling face in the dream, and it scared me (big surprise). I looked at it and said, "Give me the key." Then the face said, "I won't hurt you." Smiling, the face gave me the key that I had asked for, and I pulled out of the garage to go see my dad, who apparently was still alive in my dream. As I was driving off, I had a vision of my dad in a healthy state, which was great to see. The last thing I remember about the dream was that I was looking at this "thing" looking back at me while it waited outside my house door (the door from the garage to the house).

With so many more psychic-type events happening around me and to me, over time I have come to believe that perhaps the message of this dream does have to do with my own untapped psychic abilities—ones we all have. My belief is that I have received some of these key events to let me know that what I do with these innate abilities—again, ones we all have—is up to me. The key is symbolic:

Will I open the door? The gold key in my tire said "ESP" and was uncut. The face in my dream, I believe, was one that represented ESP. What I saw last in my dream was the "thing" waiting for the door to be opened. I did not open the door to this thing (nor the ESP it perhaps symbolized). Instead, I ran off to tell my dad, which is also very symbolic: In my real awake life, I give my dad credit for just about all of my signs and gifts from Heaven. But now, five years after becoming aware of signs, I realized that my dad and mom aren't the only ones sending me signs from above.

I have had other experiences involving keys. One day I was on a walk while wearing one of the family "tree" T-shirts that my family members and I wore at my father's family reunion. It was a family genealogy tree on a T-shirt. The reunion took place a few summers ago, after both my parents were in Heaven. This T-shirt has my parents' pictures and birthdates on it. For example, my dad's birthday—10/04 (with the year)—appears on the shirt. Anyway, while strolling along on my walk one day, I saw a silver key in my path. I picked it up and realized the silver key read: OC 04. All that was missing was the "T"—it was my dad's birthday: OC 04. I was wearing a T-shirt showing my dad's picture and birthday, and I found a key with my dad's birthday on it!

A few days later, after finding the key with my dad's birthday on it, I found a hotel card key with "Success is Key" written on it in my path (Sounds just like Dad, "Get all A's!")

Then, not long after finding both of these keys—one with my dad's birthday on it and the hotel key with "Success is Key" printed on it—I opened my car door and found a small silver key chain. I felt I was supposed to add both the silver key and the Boston medallion (another gift I talk about in a previous chapter) to my ring of keys rather than keep them in a box with some of my other gifts from Heaven. So now they are on my keychain.

Still another time, I walked away from my car, and returned minutes later to find a silver key near my car door. The key read "baton" and had "5Y" on the back. I felt the word referred to a baton being passed, but I began to doubt my interpretation after my husband and I talked about the possible meanings of finding a key with "baton" written on it. The idea of an orchestra conductor's type of baton was brought up. I wasn't sure what kind of baton I was to think about while trying to interpret this message.

Within a day, I had a quick vision. In this vision, I was receiving a baton in a track relay. I guess I found out what kind of baton those in Heaven were referencing! The signs I receive do remind me of receiving a relay baton: I don't see where the signs come from, but I trust and believe they will come, and I anticipate and look forward to receiving the signs—just like a relay baton. After hearing this story, a medium said that something is being passed to me. That is for sure—these gifts from loved ones in Heaven!

Seriously, though, I thought about it, and a few more things came to mind regarding what is being passed to me. More and more clairvoyant experiences and channeling-type events have happened over the last few years. Maybe the baton key is a message to me that some psychic abilities are being passed along to me.

Also, at the time of this event, it was coming up on five years my dad passed to Heaven—and 5Y was stamped on the back of the baton key. Maybe the message was about my moving forward—without hoping to receive so many signs from my dad and mom in Heaven.

I have also found small diary keys right outside my car door many times. The message has to do with what I am doing right now: I am writing a diary-type book from my own journal in order to share with other people the many gifts, signs, and messages I've received from Heaven. I believe leaving diaries keys is a way for those in Heaven to let me know they see what I'm up to. Perhaps these small keys are a reminder to get back to work in finishing the book!

Once, I found keys on three different occasions, only days apart. First, a respected medium said she was hearing the song "Take Me Out to the Ballgame," as she saw peanuts (in her 3rd eye), then some cartoon Peanuts characters—specifically, a white dog (Snoopy). She also said she saw me reading a book.

Not long after that, I came across a Valentine's Day stuffed animal gift. It was Snoopy, wearing a baseball cap ("Take Me Out to the Ballgame" came to mind), while holding a heart-shaped box of candy. This Snoopy was also holding a silver-gray key with a red bow on it. On the candy box was a picture of Charlie Brown reading a book with a heart on it and Snoopy was on Charlie's head. Not my usual type of gift to buy, but I bought it anyway because it reminded me of what the medium had shared about the baseball song, a white dog, reading a book, and a heart. After having so many key events happen (two of which are described later), when I saw the key attached to this Valentine's gift, I knew I would buy it.

Four days after buying this Snoopy gift, I found a heavy paper key directly in my path on my way out of a hotel. It was a gray key, almost exactly the same in appearance to the one my new Snoopy toy was holding! On the gray paper key in my path were the words "replace with your key." This reminded me of the gold uncut key I found in my tire, with ESP written on it.

I believe this message has more than one meaning. Again, Snoopy, wearing a baseball cap, is holding a key and a box of candy that has an image of Charlie Brown (with Snoopy on his head) reading a book with a heart on it. Maybe why I found the gray paper key in my path after buying this Snoopy gift has to do with Charlie holding the heart-related book. The paper key said "replace with your key." Perhaps the message was for me to use my key and finish writing my heart-related book—this book.

The message could also have been a loving one about keys to hearts. It was a Valentine's Day gift. Mostly, though, I believed I was to buy this Snoopy for the reasons stated above. Finding a similar-looking gray key to the one Snoopy was holding—one that said, "Replace with your key"—confirmed it for me.

Days after writing the above paragraphs about finding the key attached to Snoopy and the paper key in my path and what they represented to me, I found yet another key to help clarify the meaning. I had written about how finding the keys might have to do with Valentine's Day and/or finishing this book. I now believe that my finding these three keys within this last week relate to my finishing this book.

The third silver-gray key, which looks very similar in appearance to the other two keys, I found yesterday while at Barnes and Noble. I noticed this third silver gray key—a small diary key—on the rug under a book that had written across it "Journal."

To recap: The first key I found was one Snoopy was holding. The second key I discovered looked like Snoopy's key and said "replace with your key." The third key I came across was a diary key, located in front of a journal at Barnes and Noble. The symbolic key to all of these keys was the journal—my journal. And my journal has become this book.

Hopeful Hints

- *Do you repeatedly find items, receive visual images or read words that are symbolic, such as keys? Document information about these items: what they were, where you found them, and on what date. Look for patterns and how they relate to you and your life.*
- *Reflect upon the deeper message of a symbolic gift from those in Heaven: What door, for example, are you to unlock with the key you found?*
- *Dreams are symbolic. Do you have recurring dreams in which your loved ones in Heaven are alive? Are they sending you a symbolic message?*

CHAPTER FIFTEEN

ANGEL OF THE HEART

As you've read about in previous chapters, over the past five years I have received many material, or physical, gifts from Heaven, including special pennies. On my dresser, I keep the smaller gifts in a ceramic Angel of the Heart box made by Willow Tree. I also keep pictures of my mom and dad on this dresser as well. I admit that this dresser is a bit of a shrine and most of my special physical gifts from Heaven are in this Angel of the Heart box.

At the mall one day, I was thinking about the pennies I'd just found in my path that day. I'm lucky to have received so many gifts, but I had been starting to wonder—or doubt—if they all really had been from my dad and mom. However, this was totally irrational thinking, because I have received so many gifts that were obviously from my father!

In any case, I decided to ask my dad a question (in my head). I prefaced my question by saying that I understood if I would be considered totally out of line to make this request, taking into account all of the many wonderful gifts I'd received from my parents and others in Heaven over the last five years! So, I said, "Dad, sometimes I begin to wonder if these pennies are *really* from you. Do you think you could give me a penny in the next, oh, ten minutes or so? Then I'll know they're really from you!"

I know…I can't believe I asked that of my dad, or of anyone in Heaven! I had the absolute nerve to make such a request, after everything I had been given by my parents and others in Heaven, not to mention all of the energy it must have taken for them to give me these gifts!

By this time, I had walked into a Hallmark store and I found a penny in front of an Angel of the Heart statue! This Angel of the Heart statue was right next to the Angel of the Heart boxes made by Willow Tree—the *exact* same type of box that I have on my dresser in which I keep my special pennies and gifts—the one right next to pictures of my parents! Again, my mouth dropped.

My dad knows and sees what I do with my special gifts from Heaven, and so it was a way to show me that the penny I had requested: it *really* was from him. I just know that God, angels and spirit guides would not have put the penny there, saying to themselves, "She'll never know it wasn't from her dad." I believe that the "Higher Ups" (as I call them in Heaven) wouldn't do that, even if was meant to make me feel better, when I specifically asked for confirmation from my dad.

Placing the penny in front of an angel box—the exact same type of box that holds many gifts from my dad and mom (ones I've received since they arrived in Heaven)—and putting the penny there within my requested 10 minutes, was *beyond* acquiring the proof I needed to know this penny was from my father. As I've shared throughout this book, my dad will often give me multiple clues and messages along with a particular penny or a gift—all to help me know the gifts, or signs, are from him.

Once again, thank you, Dad!

Hopeful Hints

- *Ask for a sign from your loved ones in Heaven and be open to receiving one, though it may differ from what you expect.*

- *Time is different in Heaven. Loved ones answer according to their time schedule and rules.*

- *Make a connection, if there is one, between multiple signs you receive from Heaven. Sometimes the signs are connected, such as finding a coin in front of a special Angel of the Heart box.*

CHAPTER SIXTEEN

THE FINGERPRINT PENNY

Sometimes after finding a penny, I hold the penny in my hand and pretend I'm holding one of my dad's hands (I mentioned this in an earlier chapter). If I find two coins together, I put one in each hand and pretend I'm holding one of each my mom and dad's hands. Sometimes I just put the penny between my two fingers. Okay, I realize how strange (to put it mildly) this sounds! But I don't do this every time I find pennies!

A few years ago, after I began picking up pennies and pretending I was holding the hand of one or both of my parents, I had a dream visit. In this very real dream, I was with my healthy dad, and I was crying. I was telling him how much I missed him (in the dream, I knew he had passed). I described a part of this dream visit in Chapter Five, and one key aspect of the dream visit was that I was holding one of my dad's fingers, not his whole hand.

Although I was thrilled to have had a dream visit with my dad, I was a bit perplexed when I woke up. I didn't understand why I had been holding only my dad's finger instead of his whole hand in the dream. When I pick up a penny and imagine I'm with my dad, I'm holding his hand, not just one of his fingers. But then, as I said, sometimes I do put the penny between my two fingers.

One day, I parked my car in an empty parking lot in the middle of the day. I did my errand, returned to the car, and sat inside for a few minutes before realizing I'd forgotten to purchase a grocery item. As I left the car again, there was now a penny next to my car's driver door—and no one had walked or driven by my car since I had returned to the car (and it wasn't there before). I noticed a fingerprint on this penny! I tried removing the fingerprint later but it didn't come off.

I believe this fingerprint penny was from my dad. It's symbolic of him being with me when I hold the pennies between my fingers, or when I dreamt that I was holding his finger.

Another part of the fingerprint penny connection is related to a story that I outlined in Chapter Nine. I described the penny I saw underneath a huge poster in a Borders Bookstore window. This was the poster by Paper Chase of London with the large fingerprint in a wax seal. Below the fingerprint were the words: "With Love." And there was a penny on a ledge under this enormous poster (a ledge that no one but employees could get to).

With this Borders incident, the symbolism of the fingerprint had come full-circle for me: I hold pennies as if I'm holding my dad, or both my mom and dad's hands; I had a dream visit with my father where I'm holding one of his fingers; I found a penny that appeared out of nowhere with a fingerprint on it that I could not remove; and I saw a very large fingerprint on the poster at Borders that had "With Love" written at the bottom—with a penny on a nearby ledge as a sort of exclamation mark!

I believe and *feel* these are all gifts from Heaven, orchestrated by my parents, but mostly by my dad. Thank you, Mom and Dad.

Hopeful Hints

- *Look for the message of love and connection in your signs from your loved ones in Heaven.*
- *Connect the dots between various signs with a recurring theme.*
- *Be open to the unbelievable events, such as finding a permanent fingerprint on a penny that seemingly appears out of nowhere.*

CHAPTER SEVENTEEN

CALLING HOME

My desire to see a famous, gifted medium, Allison DuBois, in person had less to do with receiving a reading from her and more to do with the overall experience—the book signing, her exceptional ability to communicate with the spirits in Heaven, and the power of being with a group of people who were all gathered for a similar purpose.

During this particular medium's event, I did not receive a reading (which was very fine with me, especially considering all of the signs I've received). But, after the event was over, I did receive one of the most astonishing signs I have ever received from my father since he passed. I will share about this sign in just a moment.

I believe one reason I received this incredible sign was because my parents wanted to give me something "to take home" that night, since I had driven all the way there, spent money on a ticket, and had been so excited about the entire upcoming experience.

"Let's give her something," is what I like to think they were saying!

I feel another reason I received this sign was because of the immense energy in the hotel that night. I mentioned in an earlier chapter about how this hotel was filled with a lot of energy due to this gifted medium's appearance. I believe spirits assist mediums with readings and many spirits were in attendance that night, hoping to connect with their loved ones in the audience. Thus, the place was packed with energy.

Back to the wonderful gift I received that night. After the event was over, I called my husband at home, about 30 miles away in

Maryland, using my cell phone. My husband answered the phone and said, "That's odd, your cell phone number did not show up on the caller ID. It was a completely different phone number." My antennae went up.

While looking at our phone the next day, I noted that our caller ID showed no evidence that any call had been made at the time I called my husband the previous night. So, I asked my husband—a man who is extremely gifted in math (as well as other subjects)—if he remembered the phone number that showed up on our caller ID when I called him the night before, after the event of an incredible medium, Allison DuBois, while using my cell phone. My husband replied, "Well, the area code was 617."

The area code 617 was the area code for the phone number at the home where my dad grew up in Medford, Massachusetts! It was incredible! I was calling my home in Maryland, using my cell phone, and my dad's phone number area code from the house in Massachusetts where he grew up showed up on our caller ID at our home! They didn't have area codes when my dad lived in that house, but—from 1947 (when area codes came into existence) until my dad's mother's passing in 1976—the area code 617 was the number my dad dialed to call his parents. Now in 2009, the area code for my dad's childhood home is 781, but it was 617 when my dad called his parents at home when they were alive. Once again, I was calling my home in Maryland, and the old area code my dad dialed to call his parents at his childhood home showed up on our caller id. Unbelievable!

I've decided my dad was accomplishing a few things at once, as he often does with his signs from Heaven: Dad gave me a huge sign, and he chose to give it while I was calling home: "*Mary's* calling home, *I'll* call home!" I loved it. It also showed me my dad's humor, once again. It is very comforting. Thank you, Dad!

Hopeful Hints

- Note any unusual events that relate to your loved ones in Heaven. They are not coincidences: Those in Heaven can orchestrate these events.
- Consider the odds of an unusual event happening that is significant to your loved ones in Heaven before you attribute it to coincidence.
- Go with your first instinct. Believe an unusual event occurred so your loved one in Heaven could let you know he/she is around and there is a specific message for you. What might that special message be?

CHAPTER EIGHTEEN

RELIGIOUS SIGNS

Many of the memorable signs I have received are religious in nature. I have been given at least one "religious" type of sign that fits with the theme of each chapter in this book. But, when I think about it, all of my signs can be included here because they were initially "signed off," if you will, by God. Maybe I should have named this book *God's Gifts*.

In order not to be repetitive, I will mention the religious signs here that I have not brought up in other chapters. However, before I do, I will remind you of all of the previous religious signs sprinkled throughout the book. They are the following: finding a cheese cracker under "Dad's Bibles;" dreaming of being with my dad and two Popes; waking up while singing verses to the Catholic Mass; opening up a Book of Psalms out-of-the-blue to Psalm 23; finding my Irish names on nameplates in St. Patrick's Cathedral after requesting a sign on my dad's first birthday since he passed; discovering religious pamphlets in my YMCA locker; realizing my television had a mind of its own as it was changing to religious shows; finding my parents' Mass cards in my address book; and finally, having incredible visions: one of Archangel Michael with Jesus in a box over his heart, and a one of either Jesus or an angel permeating every molecule of a house.

Some of the religious signs mentioned above (and described in previous chapters), as well as the ones talked about below, could be from my parents (and other beloveds in Heaven). Others are sent by the angels, my guides, Jesus, and God, I believe.

My siblings and I were all taught Catholicism. Six of seven children in my family attended Catholic parochial school, and the seventh child attended Catechism. We attended Mass weekly and observed religious holidays, including Holy Days of Obligation. Actually, I can't say I observed the Holy Days of Obligation very well. I spent the day off from parochial school on "All Saints' Day," November 1st, eating a lot of Halloween candy! We were taught to believe in God, say our prayers, attend Mass, try to adhere to the Ten Commandments, and do the right thing.

My appreciation for my parents introducing me to the Catholic faith and teaching me to do the right things in life is immense. I haven't always done the right thing, but I continue to try harder. I bring up my background so you can understand why I believe some of these religious signs could be from my parents, especially from my dad. The message from my parents and God most likely is: Get back to church, read the Bible, and pray. My dad, mom, and God saw and knew how much I was in grief after my dad passed. I know they were trying to help me. What better way to advise someone—especially one's own child—than to suggest she turn back towards God? My parents are with God and see more than ever how helpful it would be for me to have God in my life.

Some of the signs are acknowledgment from my parents, God and others showing me they can see my efforts toward acknowledging God in my life. A good example of this is what happened when I left church one Sunday (described below). After decades of not attending Mass, except on Christmas and Easter, I returned back to church. (All of the signs mentioned in this book, including the religious ones, have helped me begin to attend church again.)

After Mass one Sunday, I left the church and walked out into the church lobby. There on the floor, centered with the church doors, was a dime! (This happened about three years after my dad passed and I'd been finding coins in my path often.) There were no others coins anywhere. The gift offerings are usually paper money in or out of envelopes. I couldn't believe it. I felt they were showing me that they see me.

I was moved. I felt the coin in the lobby was a way to let me know I was on the right track. The reason the sign was a coin is because it's a form of communication that they in Heaven know "works" for me.

Back out in the lobby a few minutes later, I saw another penny that I hadn't seen earlier (I don't believe it was there when I found the dime). I like to think that one coin was from God and the angels and the other one was from my mom and dad.

Anyway, I was thinking about how the dime I found in the church lobby after Mass that day had been centered with the church doors. The dime was set back in the lobby, away from the doors by about 20 feet, but it was centered. I wondered if the dime was *perfectly* centered with Christ on the Cross, which is centered in the church. When the church doors are open, you can see Christ on the Cross, and He is, of course, centered between the doors.

A few Sundays later, as I was leaving the church, I discovered a nickel that was set back in the church lobby, just like the dime had been set back a couple of weeks before! This time, I remembered how I wondered after I got home if the dime had been centered with Christ on the Cross a few weeks earlier. So I walked up to the nickel, stepped on it, and turned around: My foot appeared *exactly* centered with the center of Christ on the Cross in the church!

I believe those in Heaven heard me wondering about whether the dime was centered with Christ on the Cross when I found the dime. I believe they gave me what I wanted to know: confirmation that the coin was centered—aligned in a meaningful way—with Christ on the Cross. It was another wonderful example of communication from God and others in spirit.

I mentioned the nameplates I found in Ireland's St. Patrick's Cathedral. Another religious sign I received while in Ireland was this one. I had bought many Celtic crosses to give as gifts to others. For myself, I bought an exact replica of a gold Celtic cross that I had lost before my trip. I only lost the cross, not the chain. All of the many crosses came with chains—except for the one I bought to replace the gold Celtic cross I had lost. When I bought my replacement cross, I didn't know it came without a chain. I soon realized the reason this replacement cross was the only one that did not have a chain: They in Heaven knew I didn't need a chain for my replacement cross! I believe it was a way to show me they are with me and know what's going on. This was one of my earlier gifts from Heaven and it was comforting.

I also bought a Waterford crystal angel Christmas tree ornament while in Ireland as well. A few months later, I was putting it on the Christmas tree and listening to Christmas music on my headset. Right when I touched the crystal angel ornament from Ireland on the Christmas tree, I heard "angels" in my ears. The synchronicity of touching the angel ornament exactly when I heard the word "angels" made me feel I was not alone in the room.

Another time I received a religious sign from my father was on the last day I was in his house—the house I grew up in—after he had passed. I was picking up remaining items and saying "goodbye" to my father's house at the same time. While in my dad's bedroom, I looked up at the Christ motif behind my dad's side of the bed. Mary was on the wall behind my mom's side of the bed. I never really took the time to look at this motif of Jesus often while Dad was alive, by the way (which is another example of my doing something differently in order to receive a sign).

In this motif, Jesus has his hands up and out, in his universally known gesture. What happened while looking at Jesus is that I felt I almost saw, but not really with my eyes, my dad in front of Jesus. He was almost transposed over Jesus, with his hands up and out too. What's interesting is that my dad used this gesture all the time, not as a reference to Jesus, but more as a way to reflect "touchdown" when my dad was happy about something. I was immediately comforted and knew my dad was with me right then, and he was with God—and obviously doing well.

Perhaps you can now understand why I feel more connected with God. I feel extremely grateful to have received all of these religious signs, or gifts, from Heaven.

Hopeful Hints

- *Those in Heaven communicate using an ingenious mixture of visions, words, dreams, electricity, synchronicities, and songs—all to help send religious messages from God and His Angels.*
- *You may perceive religious signs more often as you become closer to God.*
- *Religious signs are symbolic: What is the message for you?*

CHAPTER NINETEEN

BELIEFS

What I have come to realize after receiving so many signs from my parents and others in Heaven for over 5 years is this: I believe in God, Jesus, angels, and spirit guides far more than ever before. They all love us unconditionally. They also help and heal us. I also believe in Heaven even more and feel that Heaven is all around us.

We don't die. We pass from the physical into the spiritual realm.

I believe in afterlife communications. Our loved ones in spirit are with us and often give us signs—whether we know it or not. One reason they do so is to help heal our hearts after they physically leave this earth. They feel our pain, so to speak, and send us signs to comfort us when we are grieving. The signs are given in many ways; some were described in this book.

I believe our loved ones also send signs to help us believe in afterlife communication. The signs help us know our loved ones are fine and are never too far away.

If we ask for a sign, those in spirit will try to give us one. Sometimes the sign is given in their own way, on their timeline. All we need to do is ask, believe, and be open and aware.

Our loved ones work with God, Jesus, angels, our spirit guides, and each other to help us. Our loved ones in spirit can help us but not to the point of taking away our life's lessons.

I believe there is no such thing as coincidence—our world is one of synchronicity. Things happen for a reason and we should pay attention.

Thoughts and prayers have more power than I could have ever imagined. Those in Heaven hear our thoughts, prayers, and cries. They also know our intentions, fears, actions, sadness, struggles, as well as our joy, happiness, and love. God, angels, and our loved ones in Heaven know our hearts.

I believe gifts are to be shared, including these loving gifts from Heaven, because they helped me with my grief and sadness at my dad's passing. These gifts also brought my mom closer to me in spirit since her passing almost 25 years ago. Maybe reading about these signs, or gifts from Heaven, and using the hopeful hints will help another grieving person heal. I hope so, because then others may come to believe what I really know now: Our loved ones in Heaven are just fine, can still show their love for us in many ways—and that love never dies.

In conclusion, I realize more than ever that I am not alone—ever. My parents, spirit guides, angels, God and Jesus, as well as others, are with me. I hope you find comfort and counsel from all of your loved ones in Heaven too. Thank you Mom, Dad, angels, guides, Jesus, and God for your everlasting love.

EPILOGUE

After recording signs from Heaven for over 5 years since my dad passed, I have changed. One of the most important ways is that I pray and have begun to meditate more. My faith in God, Jesus, angels, and spirit guides is far stronger.

Near the completion of writing this book, I took advantage of three wonderful opportunities. First, I was able to attend a course taught by the extremely gifted, world-renowned psychic medium, James Van Praagh. I was also able to learn during a different course instructed by another immensely gifted psychic medium, Lisa Williams. And finally, I received a most accurate, healing, private reading from incredibly gifted Allison DuBois, the real "Medium," upon whose life the show "Medium" is based. These events were very helpful and special as I continue on my spiritual path.

As time passes, I hope to grow spiritually in all ways, including loving unconditionally and being of service to others. I know now, more than I could have ever imagined possible, that I will have so much love and support from all of those spiritual beings in Heaven, including my wonderful parents. They are all behind me as I try to live my best life possible, according to God's plan while I am here on Earth.

ACKNOWLEDGMENTS

For his constant encouragement, support and enduring love, I cannot thank my husband, Frank, enough.

I would also like to thank George Foster, at Foster Covers, for the perfect cover design and delight in working together; William Groetzinger, for his kindness, patience, and interior design magic; and Graham Van Dixhorn, at Write To Your Market, for his gift of words and the back cover text.

I thank God every day for His love and presence in my life.

Last but not least, I'd like to express deep appreciation to my Mom and Dad, for all of their loving gifts—those gifts given while they were here on earth, as well as those they sent from Heaven. One of the best gifts my parents continually give is their enduring love and support from beyond. Thank you, Mom and Dad, for *everything*.

MEET
MARY SHANNON BELL, RN, MSN

As a career nursing professional, the skills of observation and documentation are second nature to Mary Shannon Bell. An RN with a Master's of Science in Nursing (MSN), she has always been comfortable in a clinical atmosphere of accuracy, reliability, and accountability. Over her decades-long career she has served as a nurse in various nursing settings, including homecare and occupational health environments.

Even her undergraduate work, leading to a BS in Child Development, demanded long-term observation and documentation skills. So it was entirely natural when, much later in life, she began to notice and keep track of phenomena outside the everyday order of things yet within the realm of the other-worldly: afterlife communication from loved ones.

As is so often the case with extraordinary life experiences, Mary's new perception came about in the context of the deep sense of loss and grief over her parents' departures, especially that of her father, who passed five short years ago. She couldn't have prepared herself for what she would see, and she certainly wasn't predisposed to afterlife communication, but when the evidence of "Loving Gifts from Heaven" became overwhelming she embraced her new experience, carefully observed and documented its details, and began to write this book.

The result is a lovingly-rendered guide for all who live with loss. The events recounted in this book have helped Mary with her grief, and have provided her with much comfort and counsel. Those who read it will find similar comfort and will be better able to cope with the loss of a loved one, stay open to new ideas, and live life to the fullest.

As Mary says, "*The material in* Loving Gifts from Heaven *was given to me. I kept an open mind while grieving, and the material was presented to me by way of signs from loved ones above. I never intended to write a book, and now would feel irresponsible for not doing so. These gifts have helped me immensely. As a nurse and human being, I need to share them in the hope they can help not only those struggling with grief but many others as well.*"

Mary and her husband, Frank, make their home in Maryland.

CPSIA information can be obtained at www.ICGtesting.com
Printed in the USA
LVOW021853151112

307521LV00021B/77/P